GREAT MARQUES
PORSCHE

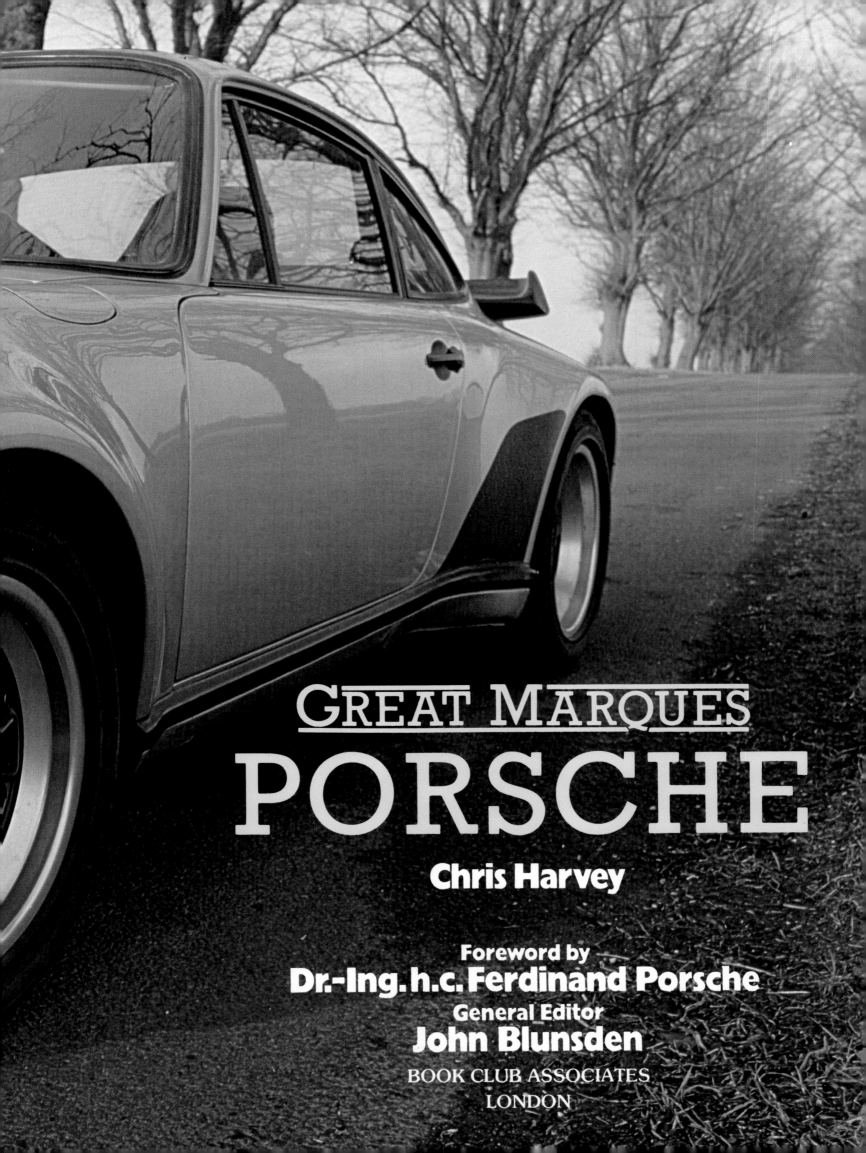

Great Marques
PORSCHE

Chris Harvey

Foreword by
Dr.-Ing. h.c. Ferdinand Porsche
General Editor
John Blunsden

BOOK CLUB ASSOCIATES
LONDON

Author's note

Writing a complete history of the Porsche motor car would have been a very daunting task had it not been for the help and encouragement of Mike Cotton of Porsche Cars (Great Britain) Ltd, and David Edelstein of the Porsche Club of Great Britain. Their enthusiasm and assistance were invaluable, as was that of Chris Branston, chairman of the British Porsche Club, Series editor John Blunsden, photographer Ian Dawson, and countless enthusiasts who have told me so much about their cars over the years. My thanks to them all.

Where possible, owners of the cars, at the time of photography, are mentioned in the captions to the illustrations.

Chris Harvey

ENDPAPERS, PAGES 1–7 The Porsche Turbo.

This edition published 1984 by
Book Club Associates

**By arrangement with
Octopus Books Limited**

© 1980 Octopus Books Limited

Produced by Mandarin Publishers Limited,
22a Westlands Road, Quarry Bay,
Hong Kong

Printed in Hong Kong

Contents

Foreword by Dr.-Ing.h.c. Ferdinand Porsche

To be classed among the top makes of car must give great pleasure to any car manufacturer—to us especially, since the trade name Porsche has been in existence for only 30 years. As everyone knows, my father and I were previously engaged in developing cars for other manufacturers. Furthermore, Porsche is certainly the smallest German car manufacturing company and one of the smallest in the world in terms of production or turnover. If we begin by considering the popularity of a make of car rather than economic greatness, to be classed among the 'great' names is certainly a compliment to the sports car, since from the outset only sports cars have been manufactured under the name Porsche and this will always be the case.

Since the beginnings of car manufacture, people have wanted to own and drive sports and racing cars above all. Car enthusiasts delight more in the sporting successes of 'their' make of car than in the numbers sold. On the other hand, a smaller firm is in a much better position to act and react with flexibility, for instance when it comes to developing a new model successfully or putting an improved version on the road. For this reason, Porsche will never become a mass producer and will preserve the exclusivity of the sports car from Stuttgart-Zuffenhausen.

I am optimistic too as to the future of the sports car— although people who envy our position think that such a 'luxury' is out of place in these times of restricted energy. As a matter of fact, thanks to its better aerodynamics and lighter weight, a sports car uses less fuel at any speed than a comparable saloon: it is 15% to 20% more economical to drive a sports car. My optimism is not, however, based solely on such economic calculations. Even in the unlikely event of the car disappearing one day from the road, we will still have the sports car. If we take the horse as an example: as a working animal it is practically non-existent, but in the field of leisure and sport there are many more horses today than ever before.

The birth of Porsche

Ferdinand Porsche was a genius. He designed all manner of machines and some wonderful cars as well, such as the Volkswagen, but, until May 1948, his cars always bore someone else's name: Austro-Daimler, Mercedes-Benz, Steyr, Wanderer, Zündapp, NSU, Auto Union, Cisitalia, and of course Volkswagen. There were racing cars, touring cars and jeeps among these designs, but it was sports cars that he loved best. His designs for Volkswagen were extremely versatile: no sooner had Professor Porsche and the designers who worked for his independent company, established in 1930, finished drawing the amphibious Volkswagen Schwimmwagen for the German army in 1937 than they set about designing a sports car to use the same basic components. This design never left the drawing board; it was called the Type 64 and it would have had an aluminium body to give the car a potential top speed of 152 km/h (95 mph). However, Volkswagen could not see a future for this product of the Porsche 'think tank' and, although the Porsche company was quite large, it could not afford to let designs lie fallow without earning money. So the firm hawked around the Type 64 design while working on a far more complex set of plans for a sports car called the Type 114.

Eventually, in 1938, the company talked Hitler's Labour Front into

paying for three prototype sports cars to compete in the prestigious Berlin-to-Rome race. These machines used the Volkswagen chassis as a basis, like the Type 64, with an adaptation of the Type 114 body design. The cars were ready to compete in September 1939 but events overtook them: war was declared and the great race was never run. The Porsche team used two of the cars for high-speed travel during World War 2 and a Dr Lafferentz of the Labour Front crashed the other.

By the spring of 1945, Professor Porsche and his team were working on a mighty tank called the 'Maus' for the German army. When the war was over they were lured from their family home in Austria to France and asked by the ruling political party to design a people's car. But no sooner had the Porsche family arrived in France than a rival political party won power and they were promptly arrested for having assisted the German war effort. It took Porsche's daughter, Louise Piech, who was looking after their interests in Germany, six months to free Porsche's son, Ferry, and until 1947 to extract her father and her husband Anton, who had been assisting in the French people's car project. She was a formidable woman, however, and it was her persistence and determination that led to the establishment of the Porsche design company in Gmünd in 1946. They set up their headquarters in a disused sawmill in the remote Austrian village and the professor, by then 70 years old, could dream again of the sports car he had always wanted to produce.

With the limited facilities available at Gmünd, it had to use existing components, and what better than those of the popular Volkswagen? As they worked on a fee-paying design for the Cisitalia grand prix car ordered by Italian industrialist Piero Dusio, the Porsche team started sketching its own car in July 1947.

LEFT *The car that started it all—Professor Ferdinand Porsche's 1939 Berlin-to-Rome racer, one of three that used a Volkswagen chassis with the body from a stillborn Porsche design. In the event, war was declared before the race could be run and the cars were used by VIPs.*

BELOW *The vehicle that launched Porsche on a post-war boom was the Type 356 of which John Piper's B is an excellent example.*

Erwin Kommenda's Type 356

This was a two-seater based on the Volkswagen, code-named Type 356 after its design office number. With Fiat-based Cisitalia sports cars as an inspiration, the first Type 356 had a tubular frame; and its body, designed by Erwin Kommenda, was the first to bear the legendary name Porsche, cast in a logotype that is almost unaltered to this day.

The Type 356 cars that followed had a platform chassis like the Volkswagen, but retained the same basic mechanical lay-out and Kommenda's distinctive body. Why change the chassis so soon? That is a question that might be asked about the myriad changes to Porsches ever since. The reason is simple: Porsche people are perfectionists and, because the cars have always been produced in relatively small quantities, it has been easy to change things in detail. Wherever the technical wizards could see a way of improving a component they would, usually after testing it on a racing Porsche. The result has been a stream of fascinating, complex and confusing cars, each one almost invariably a little better than the one before. But as their logo remained unaltered, so did their basic lay-out for 27 years: with only a brief flirtation with open-wheeled racers, they have all been rear-engined, air-cooled, all independently sprung sports cars. Only since 1975 have there been more conventional front-engined, water-cooled Porsches, and they are still true sporting cars.

By 1951, high-performance versions of the 356 were racing at Le Mans as a result of a plea by the race's organizer, Charles Faroux, who had helped free the professor from prison. Ferdinand Porsche lived long enough to see his 356 coupés win their class in the French race and establish themselves as a great force in Continental rallying. He had a stroke in the autumn and died the following year, leaving his company in the hands of his son, Ferry, with the Piech family for support. Hardly anything changed at Porsches. Production was transferred to

Zuffenhausen, near Stuttgart, West Germany but the cars were the same, constantly developing versions of their creator's original work.

By 1952, the Porsche company was deeply involved in racing as a way of promoting its cars and it was apparent that they needed a new engine for more power. One of Porsche's younger designers, Dr Ernst Fuhrmann, was given his head and produced an advanced four-overhead-camshaft flat four-cylinder unit with Ferry Porsche and chief engineer Karl Raabe, who was one of the old professor's first employees, looking over his shoulder. This high-revving engine was installed in a racing Porsche with spyder, or skimpy open, body, and the car given a new type number, 550. Porsche's American agents encouraged the production of these highly specialized vehicles which, in ever-improving form, took the German firm through top-class competition in the 1950s; and as the Spyders spent their time racing, the 356, in continually developing form, provided the production backbone and competed in classes for more standard cars.

As the Spyders developed, they became more like open-wheeled racing cars in concept and little modification was needed to enter them in Formula 2 events from 1957. These cars were an immediate success and when the capacity of Formula 1 cars was limited to 1.5 litres—Porsche size—in 1961, the men from Zuffenhausen plunged into grand prix racing with great enthusiasm. This ultimate form of competition proved to be too expensive for them, however, and Porsche retired after two seasons with only one victory of note—in the 1962 French Grand Prix—despite spending a fortune on developing a new flat-eight engine.

The sports-racing and production cars were still very successful so they decided to concentrate on them. Ultra-lightweight Spyders made the European Mountain Championship their own, as befitted cars with an Austrian origin. High-performance road and rally cars were produced bearing the name Carrera to commemorate their class win in the Carrera

Porsche road cars have always been designed with competition in mind, so that they can be used in standard form or be modified by fitting components from faster Porsches to improve their performance. John Piper's Carrera RSR is one of the most extreme variations on this theme, having started life as a 1972 911E before being converted into a Carrera RSR in 1975 for a mixture of road and track work.

Panamericana, a gruelling Mexican road race with an especially emotive
appeal to their biggest market on the west coast of America. They backed
up the Spyders, winning such classics as the Targa Florio road race in Sicily.

The 911

Despite a constantly increasing demand for the 356 production cars, it
was apparent that a new model would be needed for the 1960s. So, as
early as 1956, the Porsche designers started work on their new car, using
experience gained from the 356 series and from racing. The result was
the 901, a designation quickly changed to 911 when it was realized that
Peugeot had a title to model names with a zero in the middle on the
French market. Ferry Porsche laid down the law on the 911: it had to be
little bigger than the 356, yet carry two adults and two children in greater
comfort. His designers achieved these laudable aims, which dictated the
use of a new engine because the old flat-four unit from the 356 was at the
end of its development. Naturally, they turned to the eight-cylinder
Formula 1 unit, which had also been used in Porsche's faster sports-racing
cars. It was reduced in size to six cylinders with only one overhead
camshaft for each cylinder bank, but still formed the basis of all 911
engines since. Designs were not wasted at Porsche.

The 911 was an immediate success when the first cars left the
production lines in 1964. Since then it has been developed further and
further within its original concept, even more so than the 356. It has also
had a more extensive competition history, taking in everything from the
Monte Carlo Rally to Le Mans.

The racing Porsches

The early 1960s were also significant from the Porsche point of view in
that racing sports cars started to develop further away from anything that
could be driven on the road. To remain competitive in international
events, Porsche had to follow this trend.

The results were a string of rear-engined ultra-lightweight air-cooled
cars with bigger and bigger engines that culminated in the Targa-winning
3-litre 908/3 and the awesome 370 km/h (230 mph) turbocharged Can-
Am car, the 917/30. The 917s were extremely successful and it was only
when the racing regulations had been changed that other marques had
much chance of winning; nevertheless the expenditure on development

ABOVE *One of the fastest Carreras built for road use is driven by Jeremy
Keegan, brother of racing driver Rupert Keegan. It is a 2.7-litre fitted with
Group 5 prototype-style bodywork that was presented to Count Rossi of
the Martini company, which has frequently sponsored Porsche teams.*

RIGHT *Much of Porsche's future is tied up in the front-engined water-
cooled 928 grand tourer which concentrates on sophistication, comfort
and performance before all other considerations. The car pictured here is
a 1979 model.*

was not wasted by Porsche. The fruits can be seen today in the 930, a
258 km/h (160 mph) turbocharged version of the 911. In company with
the 930, other 911s have received more power and become more
expensive in the quest to retain their high performance and still meet
speed-sapping American exhaust-emission regulations.

The Porsche hierarchy was frightened by this price spiral and
collaborated with the company's old allies, Volkswagen, to produce a
cheaper car in the late 1960s: the 914. This mid-engined machine was not
really successful because of the excellence of the 911 series and the fact
that a changing 'political' situation between the companies kept the price
too high. However, the Porsche company was not deterred in its
attempts to keep a cheaper sports car in the range. It was decided that a
break with tradition was needed and the front-engined water-cooled 924
was brought out in 1975, utilizing many Volkswagen components. Porsche
also produced a more ambitious car, the V8-engined 928, to complete the
range, before extending it yet further by introducing the 944. This car was
part of a new policy for the 1980s of producing cars to individual
specifications to suit each major market. In this case, it was what the
Americans wanted, an all-steel version of the 924 Turbo competition car,
with all the bottom-end pulling power that could be endowed by a big
new 2.5-litre four-cylinder engine based on one half of the 928's V8.

Meanwhile, Porsche are preparing to re-enter grand prix racing with a
new 1.5-litre turbocharged V6 engine in a McLaren chassis and to
continue in world championship long-distance racing with a 2.65-litre
turbocharged full monocoque sports car. The old professor would have
been proud to have seen his name on the world's leading high-
performance cars.

The early Porsches
The 356s

The Type 356 was the first real Porsche sports car and the old professor's last great work. He was much influenced by the example of Piero Dusio, an Italian who in the early post-World War 2 years produced Cisitalia sports cars using modified Fiat components. As the Porsche design team worked on a Cisitalia grand prix car for Dusio, the professor was thinking about how he could produce something like the Italian's sports cars from Volkswagen parts. He did not have much choice really. Bits and pieces of old Volkswagens were just about all there was readily available in Austria and Germany after the war.

This is why the first Porsche had a frame made from a network of tubes, like the Cisitalia sports cars: this light and rigid structure was called a spaceframe because there was so much space, or air, within the frame. A Volkswagen engine was fitted the 'wrong way round' in the rear, with its gearbox in front of the axle rather than behind it, in the manner of the pre-war Auto Union grand prix car, which Professor Porsche had also designed. The idea was to concentrate the weight within the car's wheelbase to give it a better balance. The torsion-bar rear suspension also had to be turned round with the result that this first Porsche established a characteristic that was to make the marque famous: it oversteered. This meant that there was a tendency for the car's tail to swing out on a bend. It has never worried good drivers, but it has caused mediocre ones with poor reactions some problems over the years. Porsches have always demanded a driver as skilled as the engineers who build the cars.

The front suspension, steering and brakes came straight from a Volkswagen. The 1131 cc flat-four air-cooled engine was boosted to between 35 and 40 bhp from its normal 25 bhp by modifying the cylinder heads. Design project number 356 was started in June 1947 and the first Type 356 car ran in chassis form in March 1948. When Ferry Porsche was satisfied with its handling along the mountain roads around Gmünd, he authorized the construction of a body for it. This was the work of the gifted Erwin Kommenda, who produced a roadster with a very slippery shape that owed some of its inspiration to the pre-war Type 114 design and that of the latter-day Cisitalia coupés. Everything was kept as simple and light as possible to ensure good performance. One of its first drivers was Ferry Porsche who took it to the family's estate at Zell-am-See in Austria. On the way, while climbing the rough roads of the famous Grossglockner Pass, the frame buckled and the rear torsion-bar housing nearly collapsed. Ferry strengthened it with two pieces of scrap iron 'borrowed' from friendly roadmenders nearby.

Many of the parts needed to make this car had been smuggled to Gmünd from Switzerland because of import and export restrictions in force in Allied-occupied Austria. There was also a higher percentage of prosperous people in Switzerland—neutral throughout the war—than anywhere else nearby, so it was only natural that the Porsche should be publicly unveiled there. Early reports in technical magazines praised the car, particularly for the low build that ensured good roadholding. Soon

after, in July 1948, the first prototype was sold to a Swiss dealer, called von Senger, for 7000 francs to help finance the purchase of more parts. This very light prototype was raced for several years before being bought back in 1958 by the company for the Porsche museum, where it can still be seen. If you look very carefully, you can see those pieces of scrap iron reinforcing its frame!

At the same time as this car was being developed, the Porsche designers were working on a similar machine to offer better accommodation than the spartan roadster, which had been visualized more as a competition vehicle. This car, known to the designers as the Type 356/2, bore a close resemblance to the standard Volkswagen in mechanical lay-out. Its engine and rear suspension were the 'right' way round, which made the car a little more tail-happy, but meant that there was room for some luggage behind the seats. It was also planned to fit either a coupé or a cabriolet body. In this form, with a cosy fixed head or with a fully trimmed drop head, the car was expected to have more appeal for touring.

This model used a platform chassis, rather than the intricate space-frame, to make production easier. There was a weight penalty, but the car was still quite light because of its alloy body, again designed by Kommenda along the lines of the roadster.

Von Senger and an associate called Bernhard Blank, who had known of the Type 356 design study since 1947, ordered 50 of the 356/2 variant in March 1948, so this became the definitive Type 356. The Swiss businessmen were also especially helpful in that they arranged supplies of components and metal to help keep production going at Gmünd. Because of a body-building bottleneck, six bare chassis were sent to Switzerland to have their coachwork made by Beutler in Thun, near Bern. The mechanical specification of these cars varied as well, depending on which components were available. For instance, some were fitted with 1086 cc engines, which were popular because their capacity fell within the 1100 cc competition class in Europe. The shape was so good that a top speed of 141 km/h (88 mph) was possible.

Production continued spasmodically through 1949 with Porsche re-establishing close links with the thriving Volkswagen concern. The Porsche

PAGES 16/17 *In the foreground, David Edelstein's Type 356A fixed head coupé, built in 1958, complemented by the 1960 356B Cabriolet owned by Gordon Bond. Two of the best of these early four-cylinder Porsches.*

BELOW *One of the very few Porsches seen in competition in Britain in 1952 was this 356 driven by Betty Haig and now owned by AFN Ltd.*

RIGHT AND PAGES 20/21 *The impressive styling of the 1955 Speedster captured hearts everywhere. These spartan little cars were so light that they performed well despite a small engine. Owned by Ray Wright.*

people bartered their patents for royalties on each Volkswagen made. This also eased the problems over component supplies as the demand grew for Porsche cars.

The move to Zuffenhausen

It was also becoming imperative that the company found more convenient premises than those at Gmünd, so attempts were made to move back to Stuttgart, where it had been located in the Zuffenhausen district before the war. The firm's old works were occupied by the United States Forces motor pool, which was planning to move out in the near future. In the meantime, Porsche production was restarted in premises rented from the Reutter coachworks at Zuffenhausen, which had successfully bid for a contract to supply 500 bodies. Production continued there for two years from 1950 as the American plans to move out were delayed by the Korean War.

Reutter used steel for the bodies to make production easier, but they were heavier as a result. The lines of these Zuffenhausen cars were smoother, however, as Kommenda had been following the Porsche policy of constantly trying to improve and polish existing designs. Four of the fifty Gmünd alloy coupés were retained for competition work as they did not

look all that much different from the new production cars. Mechanically, the Zuffenhausen cars were similar to the earlier 356 except that they benefited from improvements in the Volkswagen components. The only exception was in the braking. The Gmünd cars had used British Lockheed front brakes but, now that production was in Germany, Porsche had to use Volkswagen brakes because Lockheed's German agents, Ate, would not sell the British brakes to them. Fortunately, Ate had relented by 1951 when Porsche introduced the option of a more powerful, bored-out 1300 cc engine. This engine was much superior in other ways than sheer power. It had alloy cylinders, which made it 5.4 kg (12 lb) lighter and enabled it to disperse the heat generated by the engine much more easily. The weight-saving was of particular importance with the Porsche 356 because of the pendulum effect on handling caused by the engine being set so far back.

Production expanded tenfold at Zuffenhausen and by March 1951 a total of 500 German Porsches had been completed. Work stopped for an hour and, in an uncanny silence, the workers gathered around their car number 500 as a wreath and placard were placed on its nose and Dr Albert Prinzing, who had done much to re-establish production in Germany, said a few words.

One of the reasons Porsche was selling more cars was because of the interest shown by an Austrian-born car dealer, Max Hoffmann, in America. He took delivery of three 1100 cc Porsches in the autumn of 1950 (one for himself and two for the great racing enthusiast Briggs Cunningham). He sold 32 in 1951, despite the car costing as much as a Cadillac in the United States. By 1954, he was taking a third of Porsche's production and later American sales built up to 70 per cent.

Sales were boosted by competition successes in relatively standard 356 cars as well as the achievements of the special machines covered in the chapter on the early racing Porsches.

During the winter of 1951–2 many changes were made to improve the Type 356. The most dramatic was the introduction of an optional 1500 cc engine. The bore of the 1300 cc unit was at its limit, so Porsche increased the stroke by using a roller-bearing crankshaft that enabled the crank's throw to be increased within the restrictions of the Volkswagen-based crankcase. These roller-bearing cranks were an intricate puzzle of 13 major parts, made by a Stuttgart firm, Hirth. They needed careful treatment and necessitated far more frequent engine rebuilding than with a conventional crankshaft and bearings, but they did endow the car with a much superior performance and made it far more pleasant to drive.

One of the most graphic changes was in the substitution of a one-piece windscreen for the earlier split screen made from two panes of glass. The cost of tooling for a one-piece screen had been too high until production built up.

The first cars with the new screens were delivered in 1952 and further changes included ventilated steel disc wheels and stronger bumpers. Instruments were modernized and the throttle cable, often the cause of trouble, was replaced by a rod.

Despite his success in selling standard Porsches, Hoffmann was of the opinion that the styling was all wrong. Therefore he persuaded Porsche to build him a special-bodied Type 356 roadster that he thought would be more attractive to Americans, who were more accustomed to the clearly defined wing lines of British sports cars such as the MG TC and the Jaguar XK 120. As it happened, the Porsche design office had already drawn up such a body for a young enthusiast called Heinrich Sauter in 1950. This had a normal Porsche nose with abbreviated tail and lower-cut doors. This was to be the design that became the America Roadster supplied to Hoffmann. The bodies were made from aluminium because it was expected that most of them would be used for racing. Hoffmann achieved his object in that this design sold quite well in America from April 1952.

With more design work flowing in and an ever-increasing demand for the Type 356, the company expanded its premises behind Reutter's works in 1952, despairing of ever getting the old Porsche factory back. Fewer cars were being ordered with the 1100 and 1300 cc engines, so the 1500 cc unit was offered in two stages of tune: the standard engine and the higher-powered 1500 Super. A plain bearing version of the 1500 engine was also developed, although the sometimes troublesome roller-bearing engine continued in production because of Hirth's heavy investment in it, and because it was more reliable for racing.

The constant increases in power proved to be too much for the standard Volkswagen gearboxes, so Porsche designed a new one. This had synchromesh on all four gears and originated from a design rejected by Volkswagen. The operation of the Porsche synchromesh was so good that it has been adopted by many car manufacturers and has brought in large sums of royalties to Porsche since its inception in 1952.

Larger brakes were also fitted to help cope with the extra power. Minor changes continued to be made in matters such as lighting, but the next major change in the Type 356 was the option of a roller-bearing version of the 1300 cc engine for competition from November 1953. This was called the 1300 Super.

By 1954, Hoffmann was taking only 1500 cc Porsches, so he called the lower-powered version the 1500 America and sold it as cheaply as possible with most of the normal luxury fittings as extras. This name was changed to the Continental for 1955, but had to be dropped within the year because of legal objections by Ford, then about to re-introduce the Lincoln Continental.

In September 1954 all engines received a three-piece crankcase and the 1100 cc unit was phased out. Until then Porsche had continued to use the Volkswagen crankcase, although it had to be modified for 1500 cc engines. They were going further away from their roots now with little other than the basic lay-out to connect them with the Beetle, as the Volkswagen had become affectionately known throughout the world. Porsche continued to use the Volkswagen service network, however, a vital factor in maintaining confidence in a highly stressed sports car thousands of miles from its country of origin.

The Speedster arrives in the USA

September 1954 was also an important date in Porsche history in that the Speedster was introduced on the American market. This stark little machine became one of the world's best-loved cars and still symbolizes what Porsche motoring means to many thousands of people, especially Americans. There was no wasted space, and consequently weight, on the Speedster. It had a distinctive, and minimally low, windscreen and an almost ridiculously skimpy rag top. Equipment on this open car was kept to a minimum and it used either version of the 1500 cc engine for maximum performance. The Speedster became everybody's boy racer, as fast and manoeuvrable as a pair of roller skates and even more fun. Hoffmann's sales soared with such an attractive little beast to publicize Porsche and, by March 1955, production had reached 5000, an occasion for more factory celebrations and speeches.

Almost immediately there were wholesale small changes to the cars! Porsche engineers could not resist changing things and some of their ideas were distinct innovations, sired of necessity. This is why Porsche became the first manufacturer to fit windscreen washers as standard. The aerodynamic nose of the Porsche Type 356 was so well shaped that it scooped mud and dirt from the road straight on to the windscreen. Doubtless the Porsche people would have liked to have had an aircraft-style windscreen to get over this problem, but it just was not practical on a car at that time. The other changes were to items such as interior fittings, the gearbox mountings and the oil filter. All told, they made the Type 356 easier to live with and showed how it was constantly being developed.

Porsche then went the best part of six months without changing anything, but wound up by completely revising the Type 356 to produce the Type 356A in September 1955. The new crankcase enabled the engine capacity to be increased to 1600 cc, which not only improved performance and made the car easier to drive, but also took maximum advantage of the class capacity in Touring and Grand Touring car races.

David Edelstein's 356A represents the definitive early Porsche shape with the comfortable, yet austere, interior that was to characterize the marque. A showpiece, it is still used on the road and in competition.

This meant that the Type 356A could be specified with five different engines: the 1300 producing 44 bhp; the 1300S with 60 bhp; the 1600 also giving 60 bhp; the 1600S with 75 bhp; and a new leading model, the 1500GS Carrera—named after the marque's successes in the Carrera Panamericana road races—using a racing engine developing 100 bhp. This four-overhead-camshaft unit is dealt with in the chapter on the early racers. The pushrod 1500 cc engines were dropped.

Many detail changes were made in the engine room, some of them for more refined running and others to make the units last longer. The gearbox mountings, which had a tendency to break on really rough roads, were revised and so was the suspension in keeping with the increased power, as much as two and a half times more than the original Gmünd cars. The suspension work, including different anti-roll bar and torsion-bar rates, needle-bearing pivots and better dampers, had been developed on competition Porsches. The wheel-rim widths also grew from a mere 82.5 mm (3.25 in) to 114 mm (4.5 in), despite warnings from tyre firms.

The steering was also revised to promote the more commonly

LEFT AND BELOW *The 356B Cabriolet (owner, Gordon Bond) represented the ultimate in comfort and performance for the open-air Porsche enthusiast. The influence of the American market can be seen in its heavier bumpers.*

accepted understeer, making the Type 356A a lot easier to drive for the average tyre. The Type 356A looked different from the outside, too. It had a curved windscreen rather than the old V-shaped one-piece affair and rubbing strips like those below the doors of the Speedster. Inside, the floor had been lowered to make the car easier to enter and there were numerous detail improvements to fittings. Careful attention was paid to soundproofing, which showed how Porsche was trying to extend its appeal to a clientele seeking more comfort, while retaining the affections of the sporting motorist with the Speedster and competition cars, of which the Carrera was a prime example. Bodies continued in coupé, cabriolet, and roadster styles.

The 10,000th Porsche

The year 1956 was a milestone in Porsche history. The company was allowed to return to its old home, which eased production problems considerably and the 10,000th Porsche, a Type 356A, was produced. It was an emotional occasion also in that 12 March 1956 was the company's Silver Jubilee. From the heights of acclaim as designers of some of the world's great cars, to the depths of a French jail, and back again to making their own gems. If only the old professor could have been there to see it and to have heard the factory proudly proclaiming: 'We are years ahead in engineering, and miles ahead on the road.'

TYPE 356C CARRERA (1964)

ENGINE
Type	Flat, air-cooled
No. of cylinders	4
Bore/stroke mm	92 × 74
Displacement cc	1966
Valve operation	Four overhead camshafts
Sparkplugs per cyl.	2
Ignition	2 distributors
Compression ratio	9.5:1
Induction	2 Solex 40 P11-4 downdraft twin-barrel carburettors
BHP	180 at 6200 rpm

DRIVE TRAIN
Clutch	Single dry plate
Transmission	Four-speed and reverse

CHASSIS
Frame	Semi-integral with body
Wheelbase mm	2100
Track – front mm	1306
rear mm	1272
Suspension – front	Independent twin trailing arms, transverse torsion bars, anti-roll bar
Suspension – rear	Independent swinging axles, twin trailing arms, transverse torsion bars, transverse single compensating leafspring
Brakes	Discs all round
Tyre size	165 × 15
Wheels	Bolt-on 4.5 × 15
Performance	Max speed 126 mph, 0–60 mph 8.5 sec, standing quarter mile 16.9 sec

ABOVE *Last of a line—the standard Type 356SC owned by Ivor Coverley that was produced alongside the new Type 911 until 1965.*

LEFT *John Piper's 356 C-type Carrera coupé is a really inspiring performer with its incomparable power unit. The sound and the fury of the four-overhead-camshaft alloy air-cooled engine will never be forgotten.*

As production was increased there were fewer changes in specification, apart from an improvement in the gearbox casing in 1956. In the old days, when production was much lower, components were ordered in smaller batches and as a result it was easier to change their specification. Now that Porsches were pouring off the lines in Zuffenhausen it was more difficult, so it was 1957 before there were further significant changes to the Type 356A. The 1300 models were dropped and a de luxe version of the Carrera was offered with a heater and a slightly 'softer' engine giving 10 bhp less, but making the car easier to drive. The 1600S went over to plain bearings, which were quieter, but retained its high power output because it still had a wilder camshaft than that on the normal 1600 engine. This lower-output engine was now fitted with cheaper iron cylinders, which also made it quieter.

In similar vein, a diaphragm clutch with lighter operation was fitted and chrome wheels, which had adorned Speedsters in America, were offered as options on all cars. A one-piece removable hard top became available for the cabriolet and the Speedster, and further improvements were made in the interior.

Comfort might have been a priority for the Porsche development engineers, but they did not neglect the performance side. The steering gear was improved and the 1600's twin exhausts were run through the over-riders at the rear to increase ground clearance. The underpan got a towing eye and the floor was reinforced to take seat-belt anchorages.

Meanwhile the Speedster's days were numbered. It had been introduced almost as a loss leader and had endeared itself to the hearts of Americans, particularly in the sunny clime of California, because of its stark, fun-car simplicity and consequent light weight, which gave it such a good performance. However, Ferry Porsche had never really been enamoured with the Speedster because he considered it degrading to cut a car's price by reducing the standard of its fittings. His arguments were reinforced by sales figures that showed that the Speedster, although it had become a cult car, belonged only to a relatively small cult; the majority of Porsche customers bought the more luxurious cars

The Speedster may have been cheap by Porsche standards, but it was still expensive when compared to many other imported sports cars in America. Therefore anybody who could afford a Speedster was probably able to buy a more luxurious car anyway. Also, because the Speedster's price was pared to a minimum in Porsche terms, it did not make the company much money. So the Speedster was replaced by the Speedster D, a more luxurious and expensive version with a higher profit margin. It was called the D because its body was made by the outside firm of Drauz, near Stuttgart, who had been called in to relieve the pressure of constant expansion on Reutter. It was then that the Californians suddenly began to confirm the old adage, 'you never really know what you've got till it's gone'. They howled in rage at the loss of their Speedsters and the factory

promptly renamed the Speedster D as the D-type Convertible, because it was much nearer the convertible in character. Not even this measure of honesty in using the American designation of Convertible could quell the Californian protests, however, and the factory just had to wonder sadly why this fickle market had not bought more Speedsters, rather than protesting when they could not.

Other notable changes in 1958 included further improvements to the gearbox's synchromesh, and an extra 5 bhp for the Carreras by increasing their capacity to 1600 cc, but the next big development was in September 1959 when the Type 356B was introduced. This had a thoroughly Americanized nose with higher headlamps and much stronger bumpers, also mounted higher front and rear. As is so often the case with a developing car, the Type 356B weighed more and its performance suffered a little, but at least its braking was better. The interior was enlarged at the back by more surgery in the floorpan, and a new engine was offered, the Super 90. This was a pushrod 1600 cc unit with nearly as much power as the Carrera engine. The Carrera 356 continued in production, although most cars with these engines used competition bodywork (see the chapter on the racing 356s). The 1600 and 1600S remained, although the 1600S was uprated by using the Super 90's valve gear. The types of body available were the same, but the D-type Convertible was renamed the Roadster in deference to the Californians.

The suspension was further improved on the Super 90 models by fitting Koni shock absorbers (also available for the 1600S) and a compensating spring at the back, which could be fitted to all models. Radial-ply tyres on 15 in rather than 16 in wheels were standard wear on Super 90 and Carrera models.

Production increased even further on completion of a third factory at Zuffenhausen. Reutter, on the point of being taken over by Porsche, continued to make as many bodies as possible, but various outside suppliers were used. They included the German Karmann company, who produced first the Roadster, then a hard-top coupé for a while when it was dropped late in 1961. Extensive revisions were made to the body at this time, with an enlarged rear window for the coupé, a larger engine cover and a modified front luggage compartment to give it more capacity. As ever, there were many detail changes in fittings.

Soon, the 75 bhp 1600S became known as the Super 75 and during 1962 it was fitted with the cast-iron cylinders used on the 1600. At the same time, the Carrera capacity went up to 2 litres and this model became known as the Carrera 2. Larger numbers were produced to qualify it for GT racing.

The body unit was carried over with minor alterations for the final version of the traditional Porsche, the Type 356C in 1963. This had a number of further refinements in the fittings, plus disc brakes all round from the Ate company. They were basically of Dunlop origin, although one of their special features was the incorporation of a drum in the rear disc to Porsche patents, which made the handbrake far more efficient than with normal disc applications. New 15 in disc wheels were fitted with these brakes and further improvements were made to the suspension. The 1600, 1600S and Super 90 engines were replaced by the 1600C (75 bhp) and 1600SC (95 bhp) units with the 2000GS, or Carrera 2, remaining unchanged. In this way the Type 356 ran out its production life, being made in its final year, 1965, alongside its successor, the 911.

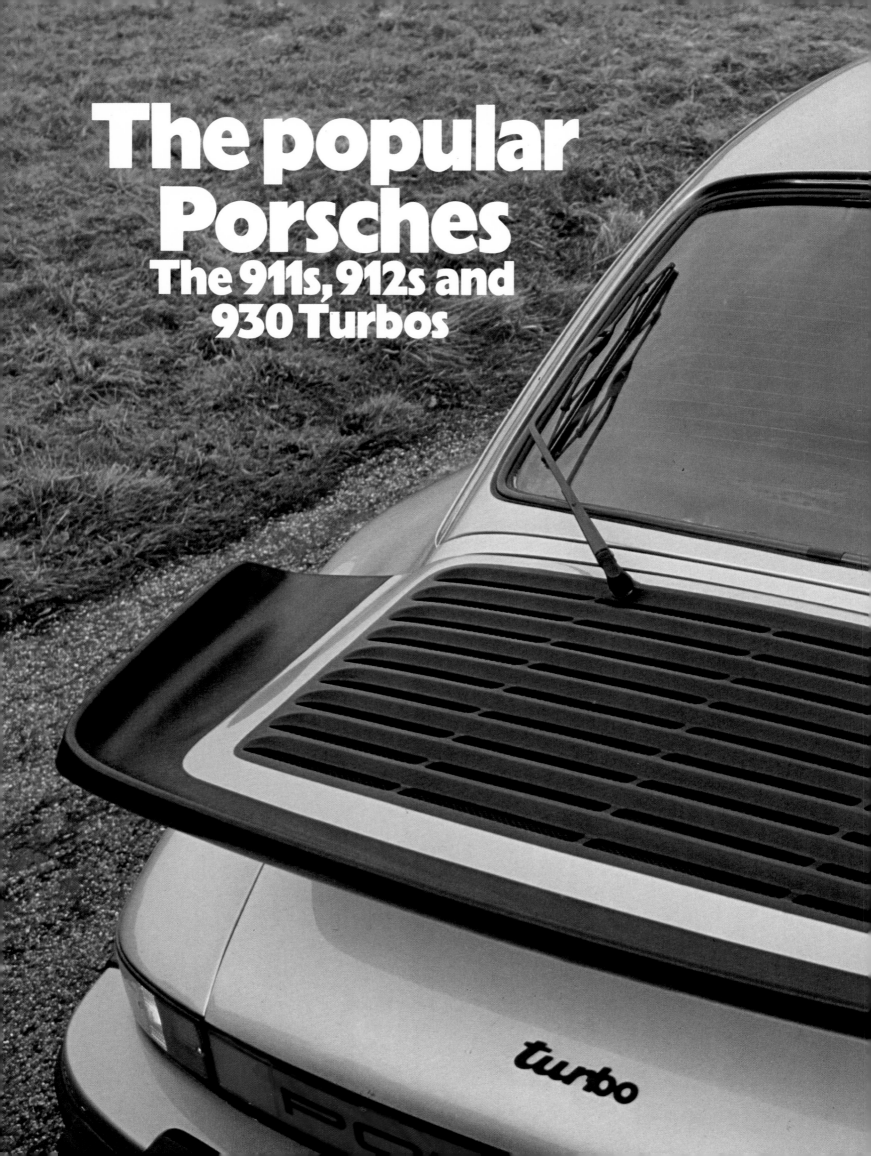

The popular Porsches
The 911s, 912s and 930 Turbos

It took 7 years to produce the first Porsche 911, but it was to be good for, perhaps, 20 years with development. Although the 911 was a completely new car, Ferry Porsche had decided that it should stick to the principles established so successfully in the 356 series. In other words, it should be a grand tourer with an air-cooled engine and the same type of wind-cheating body. The designers used their 7 years to good effect because the 911 turned out so well: it offered far superior interior and luggage accommodation within a wheelbase only 127 mm (5 in) longer than that of the Type 356 and its styling was even more attractive. This was the work of Ferry Porsche's son, Ferdinand, known as Butzi.

He transformed the 356 shape by paring away the bulbous curves and making its outline cleaner, sharper and more purposeful. In keeping with the trends of the 1960s, there was a lot more glass and the doors were bigger following complaints from Porsche's major market in America. Such had been Butzi's surgical skill that the final body, engineered by Kommenda, had more interior space although it was 61 mm (2.4 in) narrower and only 152 mm (6 in) longer. It was a thoroughly modern body also, in that it was of integral construction with the platform chassis, both being made from steel for rigidity and ease of production.

Torsion-bar suspension was retained all around to save space. The front torsion bars ran parallel with the frame and used a lower wishbone and MacPherson strut for wheel location because this system occupied the least space. Anything that could be saved in this area was reflected in a larger front luggage boot. This had to be big enough to carry a set of golf clubs, again chiefly to please the Americans, but certainly not to cause any objections from other markets. The rear torsion bars were housed across the frame with wheel location by trailing arms and a low-mounted bracket. In this way a maximum amount of room could be devoted to rear seats. The old engine position with the power unit and its tall cooling fan overhanging the rear axle was retained for the same reason. Rack-type steering was used with a twin universally jointed steering column linked to a central pinion. This made it easier to change from a left-hand to a right-hand driving position and had the useful side effect of making the steering column safer as there was less likelihood of the wheel being driven back in an accident. Disc brakes like those on the Type 356C were fitted all round with narrow 114 mm (4.5 in) wide wheels because that was all the tyre manufacturers would recommend for a 15 in diameter, which was necessary for a smooth ride.

The new six-cylinder engine
The flat-four engine used in the Type 356C was at the end of its development and more power was needed to keep Porsche sports cars ahead of rapidly developing saloons such as Jaguars, Mercedes and Citroëns. A four-overhead-camshaft engine like the one used in the Carrera was considered too complicated and expensive for use across the range, so Dr Ferry Porsche opted for a single overhead camshaft on each bank of cylinders. These would be six in number for smooth running and because it was visualized that the engine would be 'stretched' to larger capacities as the car was developed over the years. After much discussion, it was decided to use chains to drive the camshafts as alternative methods, such as shafts and gears, or belts, were either too noisy and expensive, or not sufficiently well tested for Porsche. A 2-litre capacity was selected to obtain the necessary performance.

Dry-sump lubrication was chosen because of the oil-surge problem associated with engines of flat configuration and shallow sumps. The sump on the Porsche engine had to be shallow to make the best use of the limited space available and to keep the car's centre of gravity as low as possible. With these factors in mind, the Porsche 901 engine, as it was known, was developed from the flat-eight Formula 1 unit used in the early 1960s and described in the chapter on the early racing cars.

Aluminium was used extensively in its construction to reduce the overhanging weight at the rear end. Three Solex triple-choke carburettors were fitted and the engine mated to a five-speed transaxle. The drive shafts each had two joints to provide superior suspension to that of the old swing-axle lay-out.

At first the new car was called the 901, but this was changed almost immediately—and before any cars were delivered—to the 911 to avoid trouble with Peugeot, whose cars used type numbers with a zero in the middle. The range continued to be known as the 0-series, however, and was made alongside the Type 356C from September 1964 until production had built up sufficiently to discontinue the 356 in March 1965. The following month this cheaper model was replaced by the Porsche 912, which amounted to a 911 with the 1600SC engine. This was cheaper to produce and meant that the 912 could be sold for less than the 911.

PAGES 28/29 *The 1979 Turbo, a turbocharged version of the 911.*

ABOVE *The four-cylinder 912 made in 1968 and owned by Malcolm Ricketts was no mean performer despite being an economy model.*

RIGHT *Ron Shea's 911E Targa produced in 1973 with a 2.4-litre engine and fuel injection was one of the fastest, and most pleasant, Porsches made with a removable top.* INSET *The 1974 Carrera 2.7-litre with Targa top, owned by Carole Kantor, showing its ducktail spoiler.*

The Targa
With the cessation of 356 production, the Porsche company was conscious of the gap left in the range for a convertible. This led to the introduction of the Targa variant of the 911 in September 1965. This distinctive body style, said to have been inspired by the British Triumph sports car's 'Surrey' split hard top, featured a strong, permanent, hoop following the roofline across the car. A metal panel above the front seats could be detached and a plastic rear window behind the hoop could be unzipped or left in place to prevent draughts swirling back on to the occupants' necks. In this way, Porsche also aimed to provide the open-air attractions of a convertible with the rigidity of a fixed-head coupé. The hoop had strong attractions from the point of view of safety as well. This body style has since been adopted by other car makers and is generally popular on Porsches, although there are still purists who object to the prominent hoop. Porsche sought to make a virtue out of its necessity by giving it a polished stainless-steel finish in contrast to the body colours.

TYPE 911E SPORTOMATIC (1972)

ENGINE

Type	Flat, air-cooled
No. of cylinders	6
Bore/stroke mm	84 × 70.4
Displacement cc	2343
Valve operation	Two overhead camshafts
Sparkplugs per cyl.	1
Compression ratio	8:1
Induction	Bosch fuel injection
BHP	165 at 6200 rpm

DRIVE TRAIN

Clutch	Single dry plate
Transmission	Four-speed semi-automatic

CHASSIS

Frame	Integral with body
Wheelbase mm	2271
Track – front mm	1360
rear mm	1342
Suspension – front	Independent by MacPherson struts and longitudinal torsion bars, anti-roll bar
rear	Independent by semi-trailing arms, transverse torsion bars, anti-roll bar
Brakes	Disc all round
Tyre size	165 × 15
Wheels	Alloy
Performance	Max speed 135 mph, 0–60 mph 8 sec, standing quarter mile 16 sec

These early cars were not without their problems. The engine was heavier than expected and this made their inherent final oversteer worse. The only way to counteract this was to set the suspension so that they had pronounced understeer at lower speeds, which was also unsatisfactory. Some cars suffered particularly from throttle steer in a bend because production tolerances could not emulate the degrees of accuracy achieved by highly skilled fitters in the prototype shop. Matters were much improved, however, in a rather 'agricultural' manner that certainly did not fit in with Porsche's engineering ideals. Cast-iron ingots were belted in the ends of the front bumper to help balance the rearward weight bias, and this surprised everybody by making the 911 far more predictable in its behaviour. Porsche resolved, however, to find a more sophisticated way out of the problem as soon as possible.

The triple-choke Solex carburettors also gave trouble, suffering from a flat spot between 2500 and 3000 rpm, despite intensive efforts to cure it. The final cure, in February 1966, was to replace them with twin Weber carburettors. The gear ratios were also lowered to take better advantage of the engine's 6800 rpm limit.

Once those problems were out of the way, Porsche uprated the 1991 cc engine from 130 bhp to 160 bhp by raising the compression ratio, changing the camshafts and valves, and fitting slightly different carburettors and a new heat exchanger. This is the engine that was introduced in July 1966 to power a new high-performance version of the 911, the 911S. The 911S had a slightly higher fifth gear, anti-roll bars front and rear instead of just at the front, Koni shock absorbers and ventilated disc brakes. All models received constant velocity joints in their drive shafts at the same time.

A new line of cars, designated the A series, was introduced in August 1967 for the 1968 model year. The standard 911 became the 911L (for luxe) and a new, cheaper, version called the 911T (for touring) was introduced. It had the more spartan fittings like those on the 912 and an engine like the 911, except that it had cast-iron cylinders to save money and produced only 110 bhp. It did not matter very much, however, as the fittings weighed less. In this way. Porsche had four basic models: the 912 with 90 bhp; the 911T with 110 bhp; the more luxurious 911L with 130 bhp; and the 911S with 160 bhp. All models were available in Targa or fixed-head coupé form, and the 912 could be bought with a four-speed manual transmission to keep costs down.

Sportomatic transmission

At the same time the variations on the range were further increased by the introduction of optional Sportomatic transmission. This used a torque converter like that fitted with an automatic gearbox and a servo-operated clutch linked to an electrical sensor in the gear lever. In this way, the car could be driven almost like an automatic, but the gears could also be changed at will as with a manual car. This transmission was an immediate success with the lower-performance cars and worked well with the top models in the range, but never really found acceptance with the people who bought the 911S, who preferred to stick to the racing-style clutch and manual gearbox.

The entire range was overhauled for the 1969 model year with a dramatic improvement in handling as the greatest benefit in this B series. Reasonable understeer at normal speeds was achieved by moving the rear wheels backwards by 57 mm (2.24 in) while keeping the engine and transaxle in the same place. Magnesium casting further reduced the overhanging weight. The increased angle of drive-shaft operation was taken up by new constant-velocity joints. Further improvements were effected by increasing the wheel widths to 152 mm (6 in) (which meant slightly flared arches).

Mechanical fuel injection was fitted to the two top models to increase power by 10 bhp and help meet American exhaust-emission regulations. The 911L's designation was changed to 911E to denote its conversion to fuel injection. An optional 'comfort' kit was listed for the 911T, bringing its interior up to the 911E and 911S standards. Self-levelling hydro-pneumatic front suspension struts were fitted to the 911E as standard to improve the ride even further. They became optional on the 911T and 911S. All models received larger rear brake callipers and the 911S also got bigger alloy callipers at the front. Ventilation and heating were improved on all models and numerous fittings were uprated.

The 1972 911E Sportomatic, like this immaculate example owned by Barry Sumner, is a great favourite among Porsche drivers: it offers exceptional performance and economy with a fine sense of balance, and a transmission that enables it to be used in a relaxed manner everywhere.

Handling and torque were further improved for the following year (August 1969 to July 1970) by the introduction of the C series cars with an engine bored out from 80 mm to 84 mm, giving a capacity of 2195 cc. In addition a larger clutch was fitted to all C series 911s, the 912 having been replaced by the mid-engined 914 described in the following chapter. The 2.2-litre capacity was particularly beneficial in competition in that it allowed the engine to be bored out further to the limit of the 2.5-litre classes. Triple-choke Zenith carburettors replaced the more expensive Webers on the 911T. The new engine capacity gave little extra power in its production application, but it improved torque immensely with the result that the new cars could be driven in a far more relaxed manner at little extra cost in fuel. In addition, all models could now be obtained with a ZF limited-slip differential and, as ever, interior fittings were further improved.

A lightweight version of the 911S was homologated for competition to replace the previous lightweights, which had been made in small quantities and known as the 911R. Few alterations were made for the D series cars built between August 1970 and July 1971. They centred chiefly around detail changes in the fuel-injection and ignition systems to meet changing exhaust-emission regulations.

The next series, however, was highly significant. These cars represented a distinct change of policy for Porsche in that their modifications, although still made with little regard to cost, were aimed far more at improving the car for road use than for competition. In this way the company recognized how far competition cars were diverging from anything that could be used on the road. The engine stroke was increased for the E series (from August 1971 to July 1972) from 66 mm to 70.4 mm

ABOVE *With its light weight, good handling and startling performance few cars can equal the 1973 Carrera 2.7RS. Owned by John Blatter.*

INSET *John Locke's 1973 Carrera 2.7RS with racing modifications is one of the fastest competition cars that can still be driven on the road. After 1973 the 911 became heavier to meet new US safety regulations.*

to enlarge the capacity to 2341 cc—rather than boring out yet again, which would have been more logical for competition. A bigger bore generally denotes a high-speed competition application; a longer stroke offers more flexibility on the road and, more important, in heavy traffic.

A rise in capacity was necessary in any case because of increasingly stringent environmental regulations in the biggest export market, the United States. The tougher the Americans became with exhaust emissions, the more power was wasted, so that Porsche, in company with many other exporters, had to increase engine capacity (and, as a result, fuel consumption) to maintain the same performance.

In Europe, the 911T retained its Zenith carburettors and gave 130 bhp; in the United States it was fitted with mechanical fuel injection, which produced 140 bhp. The 911E produced 165 bhp in 2.4-litre form (this designation was used rather than the more accurate 2.3 litres to link the model with Porsche racing successes) and the 911S 190 bhp. The compression ratio of the 2.4-litre's engine had been reduced to enable it to be run on lead-free petrol, which had the bonus of saving, perhaps, the equivalent of 1 mpg, as these grades of petrol were cheaper.

The increased power and torque of the 2.4-litre led to the fitting of a new, stronger, transmission with four speeds as standard and a fifth as an

option, although the majority of cars were fitted with five-speed gearboxes anyway. The five-speed box's gear lever now had first and second in one plane, third and fourth in another and fifth over to the right above reverse, rather than fifth and fourth together and so on.

This new gearbox meant that the rear seat squabs could be moved back a few millimetres for more room: this was done, with scant regard for the engineering costs. In the same way, the dry-sump oil tank was moved to a position forward of the right-hand rear wheel to reduce fractionally weight behind the rear axle. Room was retained in the front luggage compartment, where a larger fuel tank could be fitted by the adoption of a space-saver spare wheel. The size of the average set of golf clubs still dictated the amount of space that should be available for luggage in the nose of the cars in the 911 series.

Racing experience had emphasized the influence of body shape on handling and an air dam below the front bumper was fitted on E series 911S cars. This deflected the rush of air to the sides of the car and reduced the flow underneath, which tended to promote lift at high speeds. Straight-line stability was further enhanced on all models by relocating the rear shock-absorber mountings. The self-levelling struts on the 911E became optional and Boge dampers were standardized on all models because they lasted longer and cost less to replace. However, the option of Konis was still available on the 911S. These new E series cars represented development run riot at Zuffenhausen as the previous transmission's new magnesium casing had been introduced at great cost and had hardly had time to start paying itself off; the expansion of the seat pans must have been done at great cost per millimetre; and even the removal of the oil tank to its new position meant some retooling. This

certainly did not pay for itself as the tank had to be moved back to its original position for the F series, from August 1972 to July 1973. Apparently fuel station attendants sometimes mistook it for a petrol (or water!) filler.

However, production Porsches were becoming more practical by the year. The oil tank was increased in capacity as it was moved back to the engine compartment, allowing service intervals to be increased from 9600 km (6000 miles) to 19,200 km (12,000 miles) on F series cars, and such was the demand for 911S air dams that they were fitted to all models from 1973. The larger fuel tank was also made a standard fitting. Criticism of the short life of the exhaust was met by fabricating the entire system from stainless steel to combat corrosion.

The 2.7-litre Carrera

The year 1973 was also significant in Porsche history in that the Carrera was re-introduced. Until then the factory had not devoted much time to racing the 911, concentrating on more specialized vehicles. With an eye to success with standard-shaped cars in the future, Porsche brought out a 2.7-litre lightweight version of the 911S and named it the Carrera to emphasize its high performance. The combination of 210 bhp from a bored-out 2687 cc engine and lightweight bodywork produced what is still one of the fastest 911 production cars, despite subsequent development.

Initially, the production run of 500 of these cars was planned for homologation into the Group 4 (modified GT cars) category, but there was such a demand for the Carrera that more than 1,000 were made to qualify it for the Group 3 class for standard GT cars.

When the Turbo, of which Sid Lawton's early model is a good example, was introduced in 1975, it put Porsche firmly in the supercar league alongside the most exotic Ferraris, Lamborghinis and Maseratis.

The Carrera, with its distinctive 'duck-tail' rear spoiler to reduce lift at high speeds at that end of the car, was produced in three versions: the RS (for Rennsport, or sports racing) with basic road trim; the RST with luxury touring equipment more like the 911S; and the RSR, an ultra-lightweight with few creature comforts. The capacity increase to 2.7 litres also allowed the factory to produce a 2992 cc version with bore enlarged from 90 mm to 95 mm to take full advantage of the international 3-litre capacity classes. All Carreras had gas-filled Bilstein shock-absorber struts and the RSR had exotic multi-drilled brakes like those fitted to the 917s described in a later chapter, dry-sump gearbox lubrication and alloy front-suspension cross members. The rear suspension cross member was reinforced to stop distortion caused by enlarging the rear tyres to 178 mm (7 in) in width on all models. This size of rear tyre allowed the fitting of even bigger wheels for competition, the rules of which decreed that wheels could not be increased by more than 51 mm (2 in) each side.

The 911S had been lightened to form the Carrera RS by dispensing with the rear seats, using plastic bucket seats for the driver and passenger, a thin-gauge windscreen, and thinner metal bodywork with aluminium or plastic used wherever possible. Later versions of the first batch of Carreras also featured modified rear suspension geometry to cope with 279 mm (11 in) wide rear tyres that were fitted to many of them. These modifications were not carried out throughout the range because there was no need for them with normal-width tyres.

The G series Porsche 911 for the 1974 model year was the car that many people said could never be produced. Fresh regulations in the United States demanded that new cars should be able to withstand a 8 km/h (5 mph) impact without damage to any important parts, such as lighting—and Porsche bumpers have never been renowned for their durability, particularly in the hurly-burly of American parking.

The engineers and designers of Zuffenhausen had coped with worse problems, however, such as keeping the 917 racing cars on the ground! They simply redesigned the G series bumpers in aluminium to absorb such impacts from an extra depth on steel mountings; hydraulic dampers to return the bumpers to their original positions were available as an option, soon to become mandatory in America. These bumpers were largely the work of the styling department in design and it must be said that these stylists made a much better job of them than many rivals.

Meanwhile the 2.7-litre capacity had proved so successful that it was adopted for all G series cars, except the Carrera RSR, which went up to 3 litres. The 911T was dropped from the range, the cheapest model now being called simply the 911, with 150 bhp. The 911S with 175 bhp became the middle model, with the standard Carrera producing 210 bhp as before. This became available with far more roadgoing options, however, but kept its Bosch mechanical fuel injection in the interests of top-end performance. The 911 and 911S were given a new system so that they could be sold in the United States, which was still tightening up emission laws. This was the K-Jetronic fuel injection, which had been fitted to the 911T since the beginning of 1973. It had the benefit of enhancing the 2.7-litre engine's torque curve and improving its fuel consumption, even if it lost out slightly on sheer power.

On the transmission side, the clutch-release mechanism was modified to reduce the pressure needed to depress the pedal by 30 per cent and four-speed transmission listed as standard with a fifth speed, or a Sportomatic gearbox, available as an option (on all except the Carrera).

The Carrera was marketed with the option of full luxury equipment and a Targa top, and with or without the rear spoiler as some people objected to this 'picnic table' on the back.

Alloy trailing arms were fitted to the rear suspension to reduce weight and increase strength, which meant modifying the anti-roll bar and shock-absorber mountings. Larger rear-wheel bearings were also fitted now there was more power and torque to cope with.

Interiors were redesigned to meet stricter American safety regulations, with new lightweight seats incorporating head restraints as the most prominent feature.

The turbocharged Porsches

By 1974 it was becoming apparent that turbocharging was to be the best way of boosting an engine's performance without falling foul of exhaust-emission regulations and without increasing its capacity dramatically. The worldwide oil crisis during the winter of 1973–4 also indicated that very large engines had seen their heyday. Therefore the works ran a turbocharged Carrera RSR of 2.1 litres capacity in international racing in 1974. Its capacity was dictated by regulations that said that turbocharged engine capacities must be multiplied by 1.4 to give them an equivalent for

CARRERA 3.0 (1977)	
ENGINE	
Type	Flat, air-cooled
No. of cylinders	6
Bore/stroke mm	95 × 70.4
Displacement cc	2994
Valve operation	Two overhead camshafts
Sparkplugs per cyl.	1
Compression ratio	8.5:1
BHP	200 at 6000 rpm
DRIVE TRAIN	
Clutch	Single dry plate
Transmission	Five-speed and reverse
CHASSIS	
Frame	Integral with body
Wheelbase mm	2270
Track – front mm	1370
rear mm	1350
Suspension – front	Independent by MacPherson struts and longitudinal torsion bars, anti-roll bar
rear	Independent by semi-trailing arms, transverse torsion bars, anti-roll bar
Brakes	Disc all round
Tyre size – front	185/70 VR × 15
rear	215/60 VR × 15
Wheels	Alloy
Performance	Max speed 143 mph, 0–60 mph 6.5 sec, standing quarter mile 15 sec

RIGHT AND ABOVE *Since 1973, the 911 range has increased in weight and complexity but the performance is still in the highest bracket thanks to larger engine capacities. The 1977 Carrera 3.0-litre, owned by Ken Scott, has just about everything, including a Targa top, enlarged rear spoiler, and adjustable heated exterior mirror.*

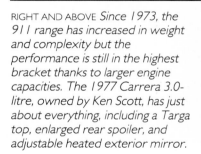

competition against normally aspirated cars: thus the 2.1-litre Carrera competed in the 3-litre class. This model proved to be an invaluable test bed for the dramatic new H series car to come in August 1974. This was to be what amounted to a 3-litre Carrera RSR chassis with a turbocharger that had been under development since 1969, particularly on Can-Am racing cars and on the 2.1-litre Carrera prototype. The changes were so extensive that this model was christened the 930, although it remained a 911 at heart and as such will be described in this chapter.

The chief problem encountered with the KKK turbocharger installation was inherent in all such applications: when the throttle was shut there were no exhaust gases to keep the turbocharger spinning and it quickly dropped from its 80,000–100,000 rpm. When the throttle was opened again there was a natural delay before it reached full operating speed again, with a resultant shortfall in torque—out of a bend, for instance.

However, the season's development with the 2.1-litre car proved beneficial in that the Porsche engineers managed to adapt the 3-litre

production engine quite successfully. They did this by controlling intake pressure with a 'waste gate', or flap valve, allowing the turbocharger to pick up speed quicker without inlet pressure to oppose it. It was a lesson originally learned on the 917. The engine of the 930 was also modified so that its torque curve suited the turbocharger, and the K-Jetronic fuel injection worked especially well in this application.

A new transmission had to be designed to cope with the turbocharged 3-litre's 260 bhp and greater torque. This was a much-strengthened version of the existing transaxle with a new aluminium casing and provision for only four speeds because of the increased torque available. The clutch diameter was also enlarged.

Wide alloy wheels reminiscent of those fitted to racing Carreras were used to transmit the extra power to the road through special new Pirelli P7 tyres on 203 mm (8 in) rims at the back and 178 mm (7 in) at the front. The suspension was uprated to Carrera RSR specification in keeping with the new wheels and tyres.

The 930 was intended purely as a road car, to help homologate a main version, the G34, so its interior specification was to the highest Porsche standards with a much-improved heating system.

With such an impressive high-performance car to top the range, most of the other changes in the H series cars were aimed at improving comfort. The heating system was revised and the 911S gear ratios were raised slightly for more relaxed performance. Sound insulation was improved and alloy wheels fitted as standard for the first time.

One of the most important features of the I series 911 range for 1976 was a six-year guarantee against underbody corrosion, achieved by building the chassis platform from galvanized steel of varying thickness. The costs involved were slightly higher, but the biggest problem with using this metal was in the zinc fumes given off during welding. This was overcome within the factory, however, and this chassis platform proved a considerable boost to marketing as well as a benefit for customers if they kept their cars for a long time, and meant higher resale value.

TYPE 930 (Turbo) (1979)

ENGINE

Type	Flat, air-cooled
No. of cylinders	6
Bore/stroke mm	97 × 74.4
Displacement cc	3299
Valve operation	Two overhead camshafts
Sparkplugs per cyl.	1
Compression ratio	7:1
Induction	Bosch K-Jetronic injection with turbocharger and water-cooled induction
BHP	300 at 5500 rpm

DRIVE TRAIN

Clutch	Single dry plate
Transmission	Four-speed and reverse

CHASSIS

Frame	Integral with body
Wheelbase mm	2270
Track – front mm	1430
rear mm	1500
Suspension – front	Independent by MacPherson struts and longitudinal torsion bars, anti-roll bar
rear	Independent by semi-trailing arms, transverse torsion bars, anti-roll bar
Brakes	Ventilated discs all round
Tyre size – front	205/55 VR 16
rear	225/50 VR 16
Wheels	Forged alloy
Performance	Max speed 163 mph, 0–60 mph 5.3 sec, standing quarter mile 13.4 sec.

PAGES 40/41 *When the braking system was uprated, Porsche improved the output of the 1979 Turbo's engine by increasing the capacity to 3.3 litres. A more luxurious interior put the car even further up-market.*

The range of production cars was juggled with the 912 designation returning on cars imported into the United States during 1976. The 912E, as it was called, was a short-lived car intended as a stop-gap between the cessation of 914 production early in 1976 and the arrival of the 924 (described in the last chapter) in the United States in 1977. This variant of the 911 had the four-cylinder 1971 cc Volkswagen-based engine used in the 914 (see next chapter), fitted with L-Jetronic fuel injection to give 86 bhp. The relatively low power output was transmitted through a five-speed gearbox to no mean effect with the result that performance, assisted by the light weight of the engine, was quite acceptable.

The 911 was the only model in the 1976 range to use the 2.7-litre engine, which had been uprated to 165 bhp, very much like the previous year's 911S. The four-speed gearbox was fitted as standard with the option of a new three-speed Sportomatic or the five-speed transmission. The 3-litre Carrera was retained at 200 bhp and the Turbo (as it was called, rather than Type 930) at 260 bhp.

The Carrera inherited the same style of wheels as the Turbo with optional rim widths of between 178 and 229 mm (7 and 9 in) and had a lavish standard of equipment. Cast-iron front-brake callipers similar to the alloy units fitted to the Turbo were used and the rear wing was increased in size in conjunction with the bigger tyres and wheels. As with the 911, Sportomatic and five-speed transmission were optional to the standard four-speed gearbox. Interior fittings were of the highest quality.

Both Carrera and Turbo had a new thermostatic heat control, which was available as an option on the 911 and altered temperature automatically.

LEFT *Porsche's 1979 911SC was a compromise between the Carrera and the softer 911 with everything Carrera except the engine, which was given more torque.*

BELOW *The 911SC as it entered the 1980s with a Targa top, supreme sophistication, high performance, and unparalled reliability.*

Numerous detail improvements were made on the J series 911s for the 1977 model year, but nothing significant. New colour schemes enhanced the Turbo's exclusive air and 16 in wheels were fitted with ultra-low-profile tyres.

Important changes were afoot for 1978 with the K series. A new basic model, the 911SC, replaced both the Carrera and the 911. It was basically the same as the Carrera except in the engine compartment where it had 180 bhp but more torque. The five-speed gearbox became standard.

For the first time, the Turbo could be driven on the road (if there was no opposition!) at somewhere near its limits when new brake discs were eventually cleared for production. These were both ventilated and perforated and had been developed from those used on racing 911s, which had inherited them from the 917. In keeping with this new-found braking ability, the Turbo's engine was increased in both bore and stroke (97 mm × 74.4 mm) to enlarge the capacity to 3.3 litres, with a subsequent rise in power to 300 bhp with yet more torque. An intercooler was fitted to the intake system to improve turbocharger efficiency, which meant redesigning the spoiler. The 911SC was also listed with Turbo running gear.

Few changes were made to the L series in 1979 other than ignition modifications to improve fuel consumption. However, the Sportomatic transmission was abandoned through lack of demand.

The future of the 911 seemed uncertain when Dr Ernst Fuhrmann, who had risen to become Porsche's chairman, said the company would concentrate on the 928. In January 1981 he was succeeded by a new chairman, Peter Schutz, a German who had spent much of his life in America. Schutz promptly gave the go-ahead for a new bout of 911 development with the famous flat six-cylinder engine being made even more powerful and economical and a fully open spyder body being shown at the Frankfurt Motor Show in September 1981, with a new four-wheel-drive system to improve handling. These options were about to go into production as the 911 series forged on with minor cosmetic changes to the M series in 1980, and the N in 1981.

The mass-market Porsches
The 914s

All seemed to be set fair for the future when Volkswagen and Porsche agreed to build the 'Fourteener' in 1967. The Porsche company wanted to produce a cheaper car to protect itself in that end of the sports-car market. Volkswagen wanted to go upmarket with a sporty image. Mid-engined cars had been outstandingly successful in competition, particularly those made by Porsche. And Porsche did not have the capacity to make a cheap mid-engined sports car, such was the success of the 911 range. Volkswagen did, and that company had historic links with Porsche, not in the least that they marketed each other's cars. So it only needed a handshake between Ferry Porsche and Volkswagen chief Heinz Nordhoff to agree to build the 914.

It would come in two versions, one with cheap Volkswagen running gear, the other with more expensive Porsche parts. Porsche would design the new car, Volkswagen would have the body made. Ferry and Heinz were old friends; Professor Porsche knew that Nordhoff would build so many 914 bodies that the cost would be lower than anything he could achieve and he would get them on the cheap for his version of the mid-engined car. But it did not work out quite like that and the 914 died a few years later a relative failure. Why?

Basic layout of the 914

The lay-out went back to Porsche's roots in its very first prototype. A Volkswagen engine was turned round 'backwards' for better weight distribution at the expense of interior accommodation. But this did not seem to matter: the 914 was intended as a two-seater all along, and careful design ensured that it had plenty of room in the cabin and for luggage in two boots. The shape was based on a design exercise by the German firm of Gugelot and was functional, if not pretty. The engine on the cheaper 914/4 came from the Volkswagen 411E, a fuel-injected four-cylinder producing 80 bhp; the 110 bhp Porsche 911T 2-litre unit was substituted on the more expensive 914/6. Both models used the Porsche five-speed transmission in modified form with the option of a Sportomatic gearbox. The suspension and steering followed those on the 911 except that coil springs were used at the rear to make room for the engine.

Volkswagen wheels, hubs and disc brakes were used at the front with special disc brakes adapted at the back on the 914/4; Porsche hubs, wheels and brakes were used all round on the 914/6.

PAGES 44/45 *Jenny Branston's 1973 914 was a really practical Porsche with its Volkswagen engine and open top. If only it had been more beautiful . . .*

ABOVE AND RIGHT *There is no disputing the heritage of John Cleave's 1972 914/6 with its pure-bred Porsche 911T engine, Targa top, and austere interior.*

The boxy steel body had a welded roll-over structure to bring it up to 911 coupé standards of rigidity despite its detachable glassfibre top, which could be stowed in the rear luggage compartment when not in use. An odd configuration of rocking adjustable driver's seat and fixed passenger's seat with adjustable foot rest harped back to pre-war thinking. However, it cost less and the 914 was intended as a cheap sports car.

So it was when it was unveiled to an intrigued world in 1969. But by then Heinz Nordhoff had died and Volkswagen's new chief, Kurt Lotz, had bigger problems on his mind. He also had a different method of pricing: Porsche would have to pay the going rate for the Karmann-built body, which worked out at even more than that of a 911 unit! This meant that no matter how Zuffenhausen pared away the costs, the Porsche 914/6 cost nearly as much as a 911 and customers could not see that it was anything like as attractive.

All 914s were called Porsches in America and the 914/4 a VW-Porsche elsewhere. No right-hand-drive cars were built by the factory—Volkswagen was anxious to retrieve tooling costs as quickly as possible and Porsche could not afford it—so right-hand-drive conversions by dealers made the 914 very expensive in the United Kingdom and Japan.

None of this would have mattered so much had it been demonstrable that the 914 was far superior to the 911; but it was never more than on a par in terms of performance and handling. Volkswagen was simply not a sporty name in Europe, and, to the Americans, Porsche meant something quite different, a true GT car.

Detail improvements were made in the 1971 model year with some modifications to meet European exhaust-emission laws. The 914/6 engine stayed at 2 litres as the 911T went up in capacity, to keep a clearly defined demarcation zone between the models, and such was the lack of demand and low profit margins on the car that it was dropped in 1972. The 914 continued in its Volkswagen form with further improvements to the

This is the car that so nearly became a legend in its brief lifetime: the 1972 Porsche 916 (owned by Ken Scott) featuring the most powerful production engine in a superb chassis. Sadly, it cost too much to produce.

engine and fittings. With the ending of the Porsche 2-litre version of the 914, Volkswagen decided to fit its own 2-litre engine for 1973. This was a more powerful development of the existing Volkswagen 1.7-litre fuel-injected four-cylinder to be sold alongside the smaller and more economical unit. Sound and heat insulation was improved at the same time and the ride softened for comfort. De luxe fittings became available as an optional package with a sport kit, offering alloy wheels, anti-roll bars and quartz lighting for the enthusiastic driver. This was to be the 914's most successful year with production reaching within 10 per cent of the original target of 30,000 units a year.

The 1.7-litre engine was bored out to 1.8 litres in 1974 with carburettors for extra power in Europe and fuel injection in America to meet emission regulations. Stronger bumpers were fitted in 1975 to cope with ever-changing United States Federal standards and more detail changes were made, including bright new colour schemes. But sales still flagged and the 914 faded away in the spring of 1976. It was a pity, for the 914 had so much potential.

The 916 prototypes

In 1972 Porsche built 11 wonderful prototypes, called the 916 and based on the 914. On these cars, the 914's roof was replaced by a welded-in steel panel and the floor was reinforced for even greater rigidity. Alloy wheels 178 mm (7 in) wide were fitted with flared arches reminiscent of the striking works MGC GT prototypes raced four years earlier. A new air dam and rear shroud were blended in to make an attractive shape. Suspension was uprated to 911S standards and a 2.4-litre 911S engine fitted, the most powerful production unit available at the time. The result was a sensationally fast car, but sadly far too expensive for Porsche to produce. And then there were the two 914/8 prototypes built for the Porsche family with racing eight-cylinder engines. They were in another world, and only went to show what potential the mid-engined chassis had. If only . . .

TYPE 916 (1972)			
ENGINE		**Wheelbase mm**	2450
Type	Flat, air-cooled	**Track – front mm**	1391
No. of cylinders	6	**rear mm**	1445
Bore/stroke mm	84 × 70.4	**Suspension – front**	Independent by
Displacement cc	2341		MacPherson struts and
Valve operation	Two overhead cams		longitudinal torsion
Sparkplugs per cyl.	1		bars
Compression ratio	8.5:1	**rear**	Independent by semi-
Induction	Bosch fuel injection		trailing arms and coil
BHP	190 at 6500 rpm		springs
		Brakes	Disc all round
DRIVE TRAIN		**Tyre size**	185/70 × 15
Clutch	Single dry plate	**Wheels**	Alloy
Transmission	Five-speed and reverse	**Performance**	Max speed 145 mph, 0–
			60 mph 5.8 sec,
CHASSIS			standing quarter mile
Frame	Integral with body		(estimated) 13 sec

The early racing Porsches
The 356s to the F1 cars

The name Porsche has been synonymous with motor sport since the marque's inception. The variety of events in which Porsche cars have competed has embraced the whole spectrum of the sport and the variety of models has been so great as to present seemingly endless confusion to spectators. From the very start, Porsche juggled engines and chassis to such an extent that there seemed to be almost endless combinations of bespoke cars. There was a theme running through Porsche's participation in motor sport, however, that persists today. The company tried out its development ideas on racing cars before introducing them on production models. The usual progression of development was simply more power, followed by a new chassis to cope with it all.

Racing started with the very first Porsche 356 and continued with the coupés, particularly those with the lightweight, Gmünd-built alloy bodies, and progressed through spyders—Porsches with skimpy roadster bodies—to the purpose-built racing cars, the Type 550s, to the Spyder RS, RSK and W-RS, right on to Formula 2 and 1, before reaching the modern sports-racing cars covered in the next chapter. As all this development went on from 1948 to 1963, the older models were still competing, particularly in coupé form with high-speed versions of production cars bearing the name Carrera. During those years, Porsches were victorious in all manner of events: from Continental rallies to European Mountain Championships; from the great road races such as the Targa Florio to Formula 2; and eventually on to first place in the oldest grand prix of them all, in France.

The factory was too busy trying to produce the Type 356 at Gmünd to compete officially until 1951, but private owners raced their cars from the start, and they won. The very first victory for a Porsche has been recorded as that of Kaes in Porsche number 1, who took his class in the Innsbruck races in 1948, before Prince Joachim zu Fürstenberg and Count Konstantin Berckheim drove their 1100 cc coupé to victory in the Swedish Midnight Sun Rally in 1950. The one-armed Austrian, Otto Mäthe, was also prominent in circuit racing and the Alpine Rally with an 1100 cc coupé at this time; and Walter Glöckler, a Volkswagen dealer from Frankfurt, had considerable success with a Porsche special of similar construction to the first Type 356 prototype. He called his car a 'spyder', a designation that dated back to the days when gentlemen raced the lightest possible horse-drawn carriages, whose progress resembled that of a scuttling insect.

Old Professor Porsche, who had started it all, lived to see his cars invited to participate in what was the world's greatest sports car race, at Le Mans in 1951. For this 24-hour endurance race, two of the Gmünd coupés were prepared because they were 90 kg (200 lb) lighter than the Stuttgart steel coupés. With slightly tuned engines and enclosed wheels, they were good for 160 km/h (100 mph). However, only one made the race; the other car, and a reserve, were involved in accidents. But that one car won its class in the hands of French Porsche concessionnaire August Veuillet and Edmond Mouche, which must have been gratifying for the old professor. He had a stroke soon after, and died in January 1952, but he had seen his cars set off on the glory trail.

Two of the Gmünd coupés also competed in the world's roughest road race, the Liège–Rome–Liège Rally; an 1100 cc version driven by Baron Fritz Huschke von Hanstein and Petermax Müller finishing second in class and a 1500 cc car driven by Le Mans team manager Paul von Guilleaume and Count von der Mühle winning their class and finishing third overall—a magnificent achievement. The 1500 cc engine was still secret then: the factory claimed it was a 1300 cc, but had to come clean in the end, such was the speed of this car!

Glöckler joined the team for a record attempt with the 1500 cc car at the Montlhéry track near Paris that autumn. After much drama with a gearbox jammed in third, they took the world 72-hour record with other records falling to the 1100 cc coupé and Glöckler's spyder. With these records achieved and a thousand cars produced at Zuffenhausen, Porsche was already powering its way into the halls of fame.

The Glöckler-Porsche was then sold to American Porsche distributor, Max Hoffmann, who raced it in the United States in 1952 as Glöckler continued to build more Porsche specials with factory cooperation for European racing. Power had been practically doubled but it was evident by mid-season that a new engine was needed to keep Porsche ahead of competitors such as the Italian OSCA made by the Maserati brothers; and if Walter Glöckler could build such successful specials, then surely the factory could do as well.

As a result, work started on the new Type 550 with an engine by the factory's budding camshaft designer Dr Ernst Fuhrmann, working under the watchful eyes of Karl Raabe, Professor Ferdinand Porsche's able

PAGES 50/51 *The Donington Collection's eight-cylinder Formula 1 Porsche, built in 1962, was Porsche's final attempt to reach the top in GPs.*

ABOVE *Early Porsches are still active in historic racing as can be seen from the keen duel being fought between Tony Standen's 356B roadster (number 35) and John Lucas's 356 (number 56) in the International Classic Car Weekend's event for road sports cars built between 1945 and 1968, at Donington in 1979.*

lieutenant from the earliest days and the new young chief, Dr Ferry Porsche. The Type 550 was the first of the legendary Porsche Spyders.

Meanwhile the factory continued to race the Gmünd coupés in 1100 cc and 1500 cc form with class wins at Le Mans for Veuillet and Mouche and in the Italian classic road race, the Mille Miglia, for 'Tin' Berckheim and Count Giovanni ('Johnny') Lurani, and private owners, Prince Paul Metternich and Count Einseidel. Porsche dominated the Liège–Rome–Liège Rally with Helmut Polensky and Walter Schulter winning in a 1500 cc coupé, Paul Stasse and rising star Hans Herrmann third, with von Guilleaume and Scheube fourth. Private entrants Werner Engel and Hansleo von Hosch were ninth and a works car driven by von Hanstein and Müller tenth after a crash.

In America, the 1951 team cars performed well in the hands of Hoffmann and West Coast distributor, Austrian-born John von Neumann. He sliced the top off one of the Le Mans coupés to save weight in the contemporary American sprint-type racing and gave birth to a new breed of Porsche in the America Roadster and eventually the Speedster, which were to be so successful in Sport Car Club of America racing.

Metternich and Berckheim took their cars to Mexico for the fearsome Carrera Panamericana road race in 1952, where Metternich's cabriolet finished eighth among the sports cars at an incredible average of 133.58 km/h (83 mph). Numerous other successes were recorded in rallies, road races and hill climbs, but really the stage was set for the new Type 550.

The arrival of the Type 550

This was to be the first Porsche designed specifically for racing, with its ladder-type frame and alloy Kommenda body in open or closed form. The coupés were faster because of their superior aerodynamics, but the open versions with their better visibility and lighter weight were used on circuits where top speed was less important. The Type 550s had independent torsion-bar and trailing-arm suspension with swing axles at the back and massive drum brakes to cope with speeds up to 225 km/h (140 mph). At first they were fitted with 1500 cc pushrod engines boosted to 98 bhp (the very limit of development for that unit) to tide them over during the lengthy gestation period of the new four-cam engine. Glöckler gave the new car, appropriately a spyder, its debut by winning at the Nürburgring in May 1953. A sister car was built for Le Mans and both were fitted with 78 bhp versions of the pushrod engine for reliability and went so well that Richard von Frankenberg and Paul Frère led in von Hanstein and Wilhelm Hild to first and second places in their class. These cars were fitted with coupé tops for this ultra-fast race, but shed them again by the time the Nürburgring came round again in August. Lined up alongside them for practice was a third Type 550, which made a much different noise. It was the first to be fitted with the far more

complex flat-four engine with its dry-sumping, twin coils, distributor and plugs, and its 110 bhp conveyed through the distinctive Hirth roller-bearing crank. It was first raced into third place in the Freiburg hill climb in August 1953 with Hans Stuck at the wheel. Meanwhile the works prepared the earlier Type 550s for a Guatemalan team headed by Jaroslav Juhan to race in the Carrera. Juhan's car was fastest on four of the eight stages spread over five days before retiring to leave its class win to team mate José Herrarte, with Fernando Segura second in a Type 356 coupé.

The works was then concentrating on developing the Type 550/1500RS with four-cam engine for 1954. These late Type 550 cars were easily distinguished by their finned coachwork, although the actual lines of the body varied from car to car. One of the early 1954 Type 550s, called the Buckelwagen because of its 'hunch-backed' body style, also featured an underslung frame that was to be adopted on later Type 550s. These works Spyders enjoyed a great deal of success in the next 18 months: Herrmann won his class in the Mille Miglia in 1954 after a hair-raising incident that involved driving under a crossing gate as a train approached; and the Belgians Stasse and Frère outlasted the OSCAs to win their class at Le Mans soon after.

The works Type 550s were sidelined by ignition trouble in this race, but once that was cured they proved to be almost invincible in the 1.5-litre class of international sports-car racing. Throughout this period, they were gradually improved, receiving five-speed gearboxes (which were later to find their way on to road cars) from the Tourist Trophy in 1955. Notable victories included class wins in the Buenos Aires 1000 kilometres; at Sebring; at Le Mans in 1955, with the Index of Performance as well; and in the Tourist Trophy. Type 356s continued to be successful in events such as the Tulip Rally and towards the end of the 1954 season, a slightly detuned four-cam engine was inserted into a Gmünd coupé with its top cut off for Polensky and Herbert Linge to drive in the Liège–Rome–Liège Rally. They won easily and this car was to be the forerunner of a new form of Porsche. The factory had to make 100 of these cars to qualify them in GT racing, so they called them Carreras to appeal to their largest market in America—and had no trouble selling them.

Meanwhile the Type 550 carried on winning in 1955, although opposition was becoming stiff at the end of the season, notably from an East German called Edgar Barth in an EMW and Jean Behra from France in a Maserati. These were to become great names in Porsche history, with Wolfgang Count Berghe von Trips, who had just started enlivening GT racing with his private Type 356 coupé.

As more and more Type 550s were sold to eager American customers, Porsche parts started appearing in other people's chassis! One of the most successful Porsche specials in SCCA racing was called the Pooper, a British Cooper 500 cc-type all-enveloping racing car fitted with a Porsche 1500S engine. This ultra-lightweight car proved to have the legs of the Type 550s in the hands of its constructor, Pete Lovely—much to

the embarrassment of the factory back in Germany.

It was at this point that the factory felt that it had to do something about the rather heavy chassis, so the engineers took over from the racing department, who had laid out the simple ladder frame. The result was a far lighter and more rigid spaceframe with improved rear suspension; it was so much better than the Type 550 that it was called the 550A/1500RS. This, however, was soon to be abbreviated to RS.

This car made its debut in the Nürburgring 1000 kilometres race in 1956, and was nearly upstaged by another Porsche special. This was an old, and rather battered, Type 550 fitted with a large wing by its owner, Michael May. The wing worked so well that it was far faster than all the other 1500 cc cars, the works machines included. Team manager Huschke von Hanstein promptly protested, and with race director von Guilleaume they persuaded May to remove the wing because it blocked other drivers' vision. Strangely, nobody followed up this line of development for a dozen years until wings suddenly took over in most forms of racing.

With May's wing out of the way, the factory dominated the 1500 cc class and carried on from there with class wins in numerous events, including Le Mans. By far the greatest victory, however, was by the brilliant Italian, Umberto Maglioli, in the 1956 Targa Florio. He drove a

ABOVE AND LEFT *The Type 550A, like Peter Jackson's 1955 model, was one of the first Porsches designed specifically for racing. Its greatest success was in the Targa Florio in 1956 which established Porsche's name in top-flight competition. The 550A's full title was 550A/1500RS.*

works RS single-handed for eight hours on the tortuous Sicilian circuit to win outright and put Porsche right among the top flight of racing sports cars for the first time.

Towards the end of the year, the factory started producing the RS for private customers, the first cars reaching America in time for Sebring in 1957. The earliest customers included Mexican millionaire's son Ricardo Rodriguez, who started a brilliant although brief racing career in an RS at the age of 15. In Europe, Barth was lured into the Porsche camp when EMW gave up racing. He became one of Porsche's best-known drivers, particularly in hill climbs. Meanwhile Maglioli took an RS to fifth overall in the last of the great Italian Mille Miglia road races in 1957.

The RSK

The works then tried a lowered version of the RS called the RSK, after its K-shaped front suspension frame. The design of this car used a lot of lessons learned from an ill-fated RS with a special low-frontal-area body called the Mickey Mouse. It suffered from instability and was written off by von Frankenberg at the Avus in 1956, and the RSK had similar problems during its first competition outings in 1957, despite the addition of small fins on the rear wings of the vehicle.

The RSK was crashed at Le Mans and used only in a few hill climbs before further development took place over the winter. Meanwhile Carreras in coupé and Speedster form won their classes in all manner of races and rallies as the works continued to develop the RSK for top-flight racing. The special front suspension was abandoned, but the K designation was kept; the torsion-bar swing axles were dispensed with in favour of a more sophisticated coil spring and Watt linkage rear suspension. The RSK's engine was also boosted to 142 bhp in 1.5-litre form with larger capacities up to 1.7 litres for hill climbs and sprints.

Behra and Barth became the star drivers in works RSK sports cars in 1958, challenging for the overall lead against Ferraris, Maseratis, Listers and Aston Martins.

Formula 2 also became attractive as the RSK proved to be practically as fast as the smaller open-wheeled racing cars. One of the 1956 works RS cars had been converted to Formula 2 specification for the 1957 German Grand Prix by the simple expedient of covering in the passenger area. With Barth at the wheel, it won the Formula 2 race after Roy Salvadori's 'proper' F2 Cooper-Climax retired with transmission trouble. Suitably encouraged, the works developed the RSK as a dual-purpose Formula 2/sports-racing car for the 1958 season. The chief competitors were the Coopers and Lotuses, which were lighter but suffered from inferior aerodynamics on long straights and did not have quite so much power. These Porsches were handled with great success in central-seater and offset configurations by a variety of drivers including Stirling Moss (when he had time off from Maserati) and Masten Gregory.

In world championship sports-car racing, Porsche piled up the points to finish second to Ferrari in 1958 before another great win in the Targa Florio in 1959 for Barth with Wolfgang Seidel. The factory also developed

TYPE 718 RSK (1958)	
ENGINE	
Type	Flat, air-cooled
No. of cylinders	4
Bore/stroke mm	85 × 66
Displacement cc	1498
Valve operation	Four overhead camshafts
Sparkplugs per cyl.	1
Compression ratio	9.8:1
Induction	Two Weber carburettors, 40 DCM or 46 IDM
BHP	148 at 8000 rpm
DRIVE TRAIN	
Clutch	Single dry plate
Transmission	Five-speed
CHASSIS	
Frame	Steel tubes
Wheelbase mm	2100
Track – front mm	1290
rear mm	1250
Suspension – front	Independent trailing arms and torsion bars
rear	Independent swinging axles, trailing arms, coil springs, Watt linkages
Brakes	Drums all round
Tyre size – front	5.50 × 15
rear	5.90 × 15
Wheels	Bolt-on
Performance	Max speed around 155 mph, no other figures recorded

ABOVE *Jean Behra wins at Rheims in 1958 to beat the exposed-wheel Formula 2 cars with his central-seat Porsche RSK sports car.*

RIGHT *In the 1960 German Grand Prix at the Nürburgring, Jo Bonnier in this Formula 2 Porsche easily won from his team mate von Trips.*

OPPOSITE *The Donington Collection includes a four-cylinder Porsche Formula 1 car of the type used in 1961 while the new eight-cylinder unit was being developed.*

LEFT INSET OPPOSITE *Edgar Barth won the European Mountain Championship in 1963 and 1964 with this W-RS Spyder (Grossmutter).*

a lighter, exposed-wheel, version of the RSK for circuits with slow corners, such as Monaco. One of these qualified for the Monaco Grand Prix against F1 machinery, but crashed on the second lap; it was rebuilt for Rheims a month later and took third place for Jo Bonnier. At this time too, various drivers raced a Formula 2 Porsche special built by Behra, who was otherwise engaged for grand prix racing by Ferrari. All this gave Porsche an excellent insight into the new Formula 1 to come.

The Carrera was not neglected, though, with four-cam engines developing up to 130 bhp. Such cars were highly successful in 1600 cc 'improved GT' classes with wins in the Liège–Rome–Liège for R. Buchet in 1957, with Claude Storez, and with Strähle in 1959.

Development for the new 1.5-litre Formula 1 in 1961 continued throughout 1960, with the Formula 2 cars alongside improved versions of the RSK called RS60 Spyders. The works loaned Stirling Moss's sponsor, Rob Walker, a Formula 2 car for the 1960 season, but the brilliant British driver did not have much chance to drive it, spending several months out of action following a crash in a Lotus. Bonnier and von Trips finished first and second in the German Grand Prix, however, and Bonnier won the Targa Florio with Herrmann in an RS60. Herrmann also won at Sebring in a similar car shared with Olivier Gendebien, and numerous class wins were recorded in all manner of events from endurance racing to rallying.

During the winter of 1960–1, Porsche spent much time on development of a new, more powerful, flat-eight engine for Formula 1, and of disc brakes, although the existing drum brakes had always proved perfectly adequate. An experimental chassis with wishbone and coil suspension all round was also built for Formula 1. Four-speed gearboxes were developed because the existing six-speed units fitted to Formula 2 cars had proved to be too difficult for many drivers.

New engines are not made overnight, however, and it took all the 1961 season to extract enough power and reliability from the eight-cylinder engine. So Porsche had to compete throughout 1961 with the old, but reliable, four-cylinder engines. The result was that the factory's star driver, American Dan Gurney, finished third in the world championship with Porsche third in the makers' championship.

In sports-car events, the RS60 was further developed into RS61 form to win its class in the Sebring 12 hours, Targa Florio and Nürburgring 1000 kilometres, with the Carrera GT winning the European Rally Championship.

Throughout this period of the factory's involvement with Formula 2 and Formula 1, Porsche had been represented in GT racing by special-bodied versions of the 356B Carrera, known as the Carrera GTL or Abarth-Carrera. These very light Zagato-bodied coupés were raced with great success until 1964. The RS61 was further developed into the W-RS, which featured a delightful blend of the rakish Zagato nose and the Spyder body,

TYPE 804 8-CYL. (1962)

ENGINE		CHASSIS	
Type	Flat, air-cooled	**Frame**	Tubular
No. of cylinders	8	**Wheelbase mm**	2300
Bore/stroke mm	66 × 54.6	**Track – front mm**	1300
Displacement cc	1494	**rear mm**	1330
Valve operation	Four overhead camshafts	**Suspension – front**	Independent wishbone and longitudinal torsion bars, anti-roll bar
Sparkplugs per cyl.	1	**rear**	Independent wishbone and longitudinal torsion bars, anti-roll bar
Compression ratio	10:1		
Induction	Four 38 mm twin-choke Weber carburettors	**Brakes**	Disc all round
		Tyre size – front	5.50 × 15
BHP	180 at 9200 rpm	**rear**	6.50 × 15
		Wheels	Bolt-on
DRIVE TRAIN		**Performance**	Max speed approx 170 mph, no other figures recorded
Clutch	Single dry plate		
Transmission	Six-speed		

ABOVE *The Carrera-Abarth was first seen in 1960. Here Paul Strähle and Hans Walter are shown winning their class in the Nürburgring 1000 km race.*

LEFT *Dan Gurney takes his eight-cylinder Formula 1 Porsche to a historic victory in the 1962 French GP. The Donington Collection's eight-cylinder F1 Porsche is shown in the insets.*

by Butzi Porsche. The four-cylinder engine was opened out to 2 litres by the use of plain bearings.

The W-RS and a Type 718 coupé (all the RS Spyders had been Type 718s) were modified to take the new eight-cylinder engine, in 2-litre form, for its debut in the Targa Florio in 1962. The W-RS, driven by Gurney and Bonnier, crashed, so Bonnier replaced Graham Hill in the coupé shared with Sicilian Targa specialist Nino Vaccarella to take third place.

The eight-cylinder engine was sleeved down to 1.5 litres for Formula 1 (the Type 804) for Gurney and Bonnier to use at Zandvoort in May. The latest chassis used wishbones with the more familiar torsion-bars now. However, Porsche's new engine had come too late, for Coventry-Climax (in Lotus and Cooper cars), BRM and Ferrari engines were now developing at least as much as its 180 bhp. Gurney managed one victory in the French Grand Prix when faster cars dropped out, but usually the Formula 1 Porsches were outclassed by Lotus with its new monocoque 25, BRM with its reliable engines, or the durable Ferraris. Despite being regarded as the fastest driver of 1962 with Lotus's Jim Clark, Gurney could only finish fifth in the world championship, and Bonnier was 15th.

Porsche withdraws from GP racing
Porsche, who had spent a fortune on development, realized that at least another 10 per cent power was needed, which could not be justified on cost, so they quit grand prix racing at the end of the season and concentrated again on sports-car and GT events.

Redundant works cars had been sold to private entrants at the start of the 1962 season, including Count Carel Godin de Beaufort. This popular playboy picked up a few world championship points during the season and continued in Formula 1 with a two-car Porsche team for himself and Gerhard Mitter in 1963. He remained faithful to the marque until he died in a crash at the Nürburgring in 1964. All grand prix racing men mourned his death, remembering a popular driver with a great sense of humour.

Meanwhile the Carreras went up to 2 litres and became known as the Carrera 2. Porsche also looked long and hard at the success of ultra-lightweight sports cars such as Lotus and Elva, which were mopping up races in America. This led to the installation of a flat-four Spyder engine in the latest British Elva chassis in 1963. These cars were immediately successful in America and by the 1964 season, 15 had been sold, with one finishing second in the European Mountain Championship with Herbert Müller at the wheel. Barth won the championship in 1963 and 1964 in the W-RS, which the mechanics called affectionately Grossmutter, ('Grandmother'), because it had seen so much service. Tragically, Barth died of cancer in 1965, but his old favourite, the Grossmutter, was rebuilt to stand in the Porsche Museum as a memorial to him. By then another new generation of Porsche sports cars had been born, heralded by the Type 904 described in the next chapter.

The world-beating racing Porsches
The 904s to the 936s

Porsche competition activities continued on three planes from 1964: the 904 and 911 were in racing and rallying; various hill-climbing cars were developed as circuit racers up to 3 litres; and the 917 was in the top classes. The 917 stands alone as a 12-cylinder Porsche, and will be described in the next chapter. The 904 represented a complete breakaway from established Porsche tradition in that it used a hefty box-frame chassis with a glassfibre body bonded to it. This beautiful new car, the work of Butzi Porsche, was at first intended to have the production six-cylinder engine that was to go into the 911 model, ahead of its rear axle. Most early examples had the existing four-cylinder engine, however, although works cars were fitted with either the new six-cylinder unit or the eight-cylinder racing engine. Sufficient were built bearing the Carrera GTS label to qualify for GT racing and won their second race—the Targa Florio—when the front-line 1963 model Spyders fell by the wayside in 1964. Colin Davis and Antonio Pucci were first with Linge and Balzarini second in another 904. From then on, the 904 was to prove outstandingly reliable, dominating the 2-litre classes in endurance racing.

Another facet of this lovely car's character was revealed when Eugen Böhringer took a four-cylinder 904 to second place on snow in the Monte Carlo Rally in 1965, much to everybody's surprise. Until then this production GT had been considered only a fair-weather racer, although a lot of the credit must be given to Böhringer's inspired and skilful driving. A spyder version was also built for 1965, taking second place to Vaccarella's Ferrari in the Targa Florio for Davis and Mitter before it was written off at the Nürburgring. The eight-cylinder engine was normally reserved for short- and medium-distance events, the six-cylinder for long-distance races such as Le Mans, where 904/6s finished fourth and fifth in 1965. However, this car, with its outstanding roadholding, was really at its best in slower events such as the Targa Florio.

Meanwhile the 911 was also developed for competition with engineers Linge and Peter Falk taking it to a 2-litre class win in the 1965 Monte Carlo Rally on its debut. And a new man took charge of Porsche racing and competition development, Ferdinand Piech, son of Ferry Porsche's sister, Louise. One of his first projects in his new job was a hill-climb car, which was built in three weeks flat when Ferrari looked like dominating the 1965 European Mountain Championship. It was an ultra-lightweight spyder with a spaceframe and 240 bhp version of the eight-cylinder engine. To take advantage of the latest tyre technology, 13 in wheels were used. As these were not available at Weissach at the time, a complete set, with suspension uprights, was bought from the Lotus team after the German Grand Prix. This car made its debut at the Ollon-Villars hill climb, but failed to halt the march of Lodovico Scarfiotti's Ferrari Dino. However, it did start a whole new trend in Porsche sports-racing cars.

This spaceframe was used as the basis of the Carrera 6, or Type 906, introduced in 1966. It had the 904's suspension and a similar-shaped glassfibre body with gullwing doors, and was designed to accept either a 210 bhp six- or a 260 bhp eight-cylinder engine in 2.2-litre form. This car proved highly successful, winning the Daytona 24-hour race on its first outing for Herrmann and Linge, the Targa Florio for Willy Mairesse and Müller, and finished fourth, fifth, sixth and seventh at Le Mans behind the all-conquering 7-litre Fords. Mitter drove a stiffened, wider-tracked version called the Type 910 in the European Mountain Championship, and managed to regain his title from Scarfiotti. Later developments of this 910 used aluminium spaceframes: Piech's philosophy was to reduce weight by any means possible and then worry about the power.

The 911 continued to be successful in rallying, leading to the development of the 911S in 1966 and the start of a big rally programme for 1967, spearheaded by the crack British team of Vic Elford and David Stone. This pairing won their class in the 1967 Monte Carlo Rally, with outright victories in the German Rally, the Tulip Rally and the Geneva Rally, and Sobieslaw Zasada won his home Polish Rally in a 911S. These cars were also raced successfully in Sportomatic form to win the Marathon de la Route, an 84-hour successor to the Liège–Rome–Liège Rally at the Nürburgring. Elford combined with Herrmann and Jochen Neerpasch for this event.

The 910 battled with limited success against 4-litre Ferraris and 7-litre Fords and Chaparrals at the start of 1967; the biggest effort was reserved for the Targa Florio where handling and nimble manoeuvrability were at a premium. Porsche 910s made a clean sweep in the 1967 event: Paul Hawkins and Rolf Stommelen won in an eight-cylinder fuel-injection car from Leo Cella and Gianpere Biscaldi's six and Neerpasch and Elford in another six. They also took the first four places in the Nürburgring 1000 kilometres, with Joe Buzzetta and Gerhard Koch winning after faster cars, such as a Lola Aston Martin and a Chaparral, retired in company with two works Porsches. A further-improved version of the 910, the Type 907, made its debut at Le Mans. It had a smaller frontal area, ventilated disc brakes like those first used on Stommelen's car at the Nürburgring, and right-hand drive: for the first time on a works Porsche. The change was to enable the drivers to place their cars better on the normal right-hand direction on racing circuits.

The Le Mans 907, driven by Jo Siffert and Herrmann, finished fifth; it had a 2-litre six-cylinder engine, although the 907 chiefly used the eight-

PAGES 60/61 *Porsche 935s dominated Le Mans in 1979 with Klaus Ludwig and the Whittington brothers winning. The 935/77A pictured here, driven by Jarier, Townsend and Touroul, was eliminated.*

RIGHT *The 906 was one of Porsche's most successful racing cars, winning the Targa Florio and Daytona 24 hrs. This car belongs to Martin Hone.*

BELOW *Porsche 904s finished first and second in the Targa Florio in 1964. This car, driven by Balzarini and Linge, came second.*

TYPE 904 CARRERA GTS (1965)	
ENGINE	
Type	Flat, air-cooled
No. of cylinders	4
Bore/stroke mm	92 × 74
Displacement cc	1966
Valve operation	Four overhead camshafts
Sparkplugs per cyl.	1
Compression ratio	9.8:1
Induction	Two Weber 46 IDM carburettors
BHP	198 at 7200 rpm
DRIVE TRAIN	
Clutch	Single dry plate
Transmission	Five-speed and reverse
CHASSIS	
Frame	Pressed steel, glassfibre body bonded on
Wheelbase mm	2300
Track – front mm	1314
rear mm	1312
Suspension – front	Independent wishbone and coil, anti-roll bar
rear	Independent wishbone and coil, anti-roll bar, radius rods
Brakes	Discs all round
Tyre size – front	5.00 × 15
rear	5.50 × 15
Wheels	Bolt-on 5–7 in rims
Performance	Max speed 163 mph, 0–60 mph 5.3 sec, standing quarter mile 14.2 sec

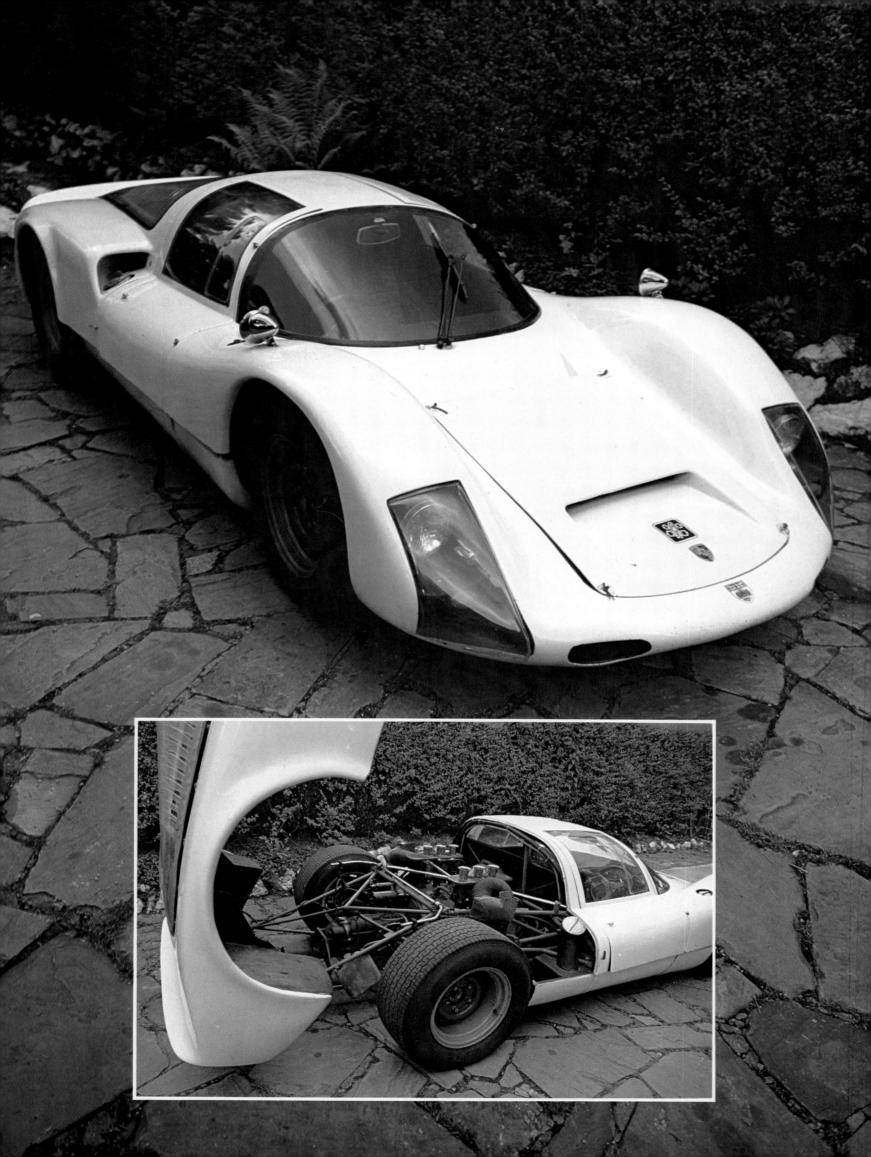

ABOVE *The long-tailed 906/6 coupé, driven by Jo Siffert and Colin Davis, is prepared for the start at Le Mans in 1966 when it finished fourth behind three 7-litre Fords.*

LEFT *Udo Schutz and Joe Buzzetta sweep to victory in the Nürburgring 1000 kilometres in 1967 with their Porsche 910/6. Similar cars took the next three places.*

cylinder unit. Type 910s in this form went on to first and second places at Mugello for Mitter and Udo Schutz, and Stommelen and Neerpasch; and a new lightweight version of the 911, the 911R, finished third in the hands of Elford and Gijs van Lennep. Porsche had picked up so many points in the World Sports Car Championship that the 2.2-litre cars stood a chance of taking the title in the final round, the BOAC 500 at Brands Hatch, if they beat the Ferraris. Chaparral won, but Chris Amon and Jackie Stewart in a Ferrari just pipped Siffert and Bruce McLaren's 910 to take the championship. In the mountains, Mitter won his second title in the 910 prototype.

The great rallying successes

The next three years were golden for Porsche in international rallying. Elford and Stone started by winning the Monte Carlo in 1968 from team mates Pauli Toivonen and Martti Tiukkanen. This year also saw Björn Waldegård emerge as a major force in Porsche rallying with a victory in the Swedish Rally. Numerous other top events fell to the 911S, and 911Rs driven by Erwin Kremer/Helmut Kelleners and Willi Kauhsen won the Spa 24-hour, and Glemser and Kauhsen took the Marathon de la Route.

No sooner had Elford won the Monte Carlo Rally than he was off to Daytona for the 24-hour race, which he won in a 907 with Neerpasch. Siffert, Herrmann and Stommelen were second in a 907 with Buzzetta and Jo Schlesser third in another 907. Siffert and Herrmann, followed by Elford and Neerpasch, repeated the success in 907s at Sebring—and all looked well for the 1968 World Sports Car Championship. But then everything started to go wrong and John Wyer's team of Gulf Ford GT40s beat the 907s by 22 seconds at Brands Hatch. A new car, called the 908, was introduced with a 3-litre version of the 2.2-litre 'production' six-cylinder unit in a similar chassis to the 907, but it proved to be no faster. It was, however, the first time that Porsche had produced a car to take advantage of the full capacity limit for international sports-car racing: at that time 3 litres for prototypes and 5 litres for 'stock block' cars.

Elford lost time with a puncture in the Targa Florio but produced one

LEFT *Sideways as ever, Vic Elford wins the Monte Carlo Rally in 1968 with his 911T fitted with 911S Rallysport gear—a car that was to take Porsche to numerous rally successes.*

ABOVE LEFT *Vic Elford and Richard Attwood take their 908/2 to second place in the BOAC 500-mile race at Brands Hatch in 1969. Similar cars finished first, third and sixth, giving the marque the World Championship of Makes title following more victories.*

of his most brilliant drives to make up 16 minutes and overtake all the Porsches and Alfa Romeos to win in a 907. He was on winning form again in the Nürburgring 1000 kilometre race with Siffert but wheel-bearing trouble laid Porsches low for the rest of the 1968 season with the result that they were beaten in the premier event at Le Mans by Wyer's team and lost the world title to them as well. The only bright spot that they could see, apart from the continuing success of the 911S and 911R, was when Mitter won the European Mountain Championship for the third consecutive time in an ultra-lightweight development of the 908, called the Type 909 Bergspyder ('mountain spyder'). This had a 2-litre engine, the maximum allowed in this form of racing.

The 911 continued to be just as successful in rallying, winning the Monte Carlo for a second time in 1969, in the hands of Waldegård and Lars Helmer with Gérard Larrousse and Jean-Claude Perramond second; Waldegård went on to win the Swedish Rally again and the 911Rs won the GT category at Daytona and Sebring. Long-tailed works 908s looked as though they would dominate Daytona until an alloy gear gave way in the engines of all five cars entered. Further trouble struck another version of the 908, an ultra-lightweight spyder, similar to the 909, at Sebring. Four out of the five cars entered suffered from suspension trouble with Stommelen struggling home in third place behind the inevitable Wyer GT40 and a new V12 Ferrari.

However, at the Brands Hatch 500 Porsche 908/2s swept in 1–2–3 in front of Chris Amon and Pedro Rodriguez's Ferrari. The winning car was driven by Siffert and Brian Redman, a combination that was to win four other top-line races that year. They next won again in the long-tailed 908/2 at Monza before Schutz and Mitter won the Targa Florio for Porsche for the ninth time in a 908 spyder.

The 917 made its debut in the next event at Spa, but it was far from fully developed, so the 908 remained as Porsche's front-line car. Siffert had put the 917 on pole position, but decided to race the 908 with Redman, in long-tailed form. A revised spyder body with flatter profile, nicknamed the Sole, appeared next at the Nürburgring, with Siffert and Redman taking it to victory. By then this wonderfully successful combination had done enough to win the World Sports Car Championship for Porsche, so all eyes were turned on Le Mans to see if they could win again. This time the leading Porsches ran into trouble and a Wyer GT40 driven by Jacky Ickx and Jackie Oliver scraped home 200 yards ahead of Herrmann and Larrousse's 908 after a thrilling battle over the last three hours.

The Porsche hierarchy was shocked at having been drubbed by a relatively old Ford GT40, so promptly gave up and arranged for Wyer to run the team next year! In the meantime, the works Porsche 908s were handed over to the private Porsche Salzburg team to complete the season; Siffert and Redman won in one of these cars at Watkins Glen.

There seemed to be no stopping the 911s either. Waldegård and Helmer won the Monte Carlo Rally again in 1970—the second time for them and the third for Porsche—and repeated this feat in the Swedish Rally. The 914 was also prepared for racing in an attempt to boost sales. Three teams competed with success in SCCA racing and a much-modified 914/6 GT model was built by the factory for European events. Apart from keeping to the car's homologated 2-litre capacity and Weber carburation, the specification was brought up to Carrera 6 standards. These cars were immediately successful: one example entered by Auguste Veuillet's Parisian Porsche dealership finished sixth at Le Mans as less reliable cars fell out. The drivers were Guy Chasseuil and Claude Ballot-Lena. Larrousse, Claude Haldi and Helmut Marko also won the Marathon de la Route in a 914/6 GT.

The Type 908/3

Meanwhile Wyer took over the big sports cars, with the 917 as a front runner. It was felt, however, that a 908, or an even lighter version of it, would be at an advantage on tricky circuits such as that used for the Targa Florio. The works, therefore, developed the 909 with a 908 engine for Wyer, and called this model the 908/3. It was similar to the 909 in that it had an alloy tube frame, but the 3-litre power train's differential was mounted behind the gearbox to make the car more manoeuvrable on tight corners. To compensate for this extra swinging weight, the driver was moved forward. Three of these cars were sent to Sicily for Wyer's team with a fourth for Porsche Salzburg. Seven 908/2s also competed as more than a dozen had been sold to private entrants by then. Siffert and Redman were on top form and led in Wyer team mates Rodriguez and Leo Kinnunen, with the third Wyer car, driven by Richard Attwood and Waldegård, sixth. Not to be outdone, a private 908/2, driven by Hans

TYPE 908/4 (1975)

ENGINE

Type	Flat, air-cooled
No. of cylinders	6
Bore/stroke mm	83 × 66
Displacement cc	2997
Valve operation	Two overhead camshafts
Sparkplugs per cyl.	2
Compression ratio	6.5:1
Induction	Bosch fuel injection with turbocharger
BHP	516 at 7600 rpm

DRIVE TRAIN

Clutch	Triple plate
Transmission	Five-speed

CHASSIS

Frame	Alloy tubular as 908/3
Wheelbase mm	2300
Track – front mm	1504
rear mm	1510
Suspension – front	Independent wishbone and coil, anti-roll bar
rear	Independent wishbone and coil, radius arms, anti-roll bar
Brakes	Ventilated disc all round
Tyre size – front	9.5 × 13
rear	14.5 × 13
Wheels	Bolt-on
Performance	Max speed around 200 mph. No other figures recorded

Laine and van Lennep finished fourth after losing a front wheel at one point. With an incredible display of driving ability, Laine accelerated to 225 km/h (140 mph) on three wheels, lifting the nose sufficiently to reach the pits for a new wheel! Unfortunately this brilliant Finnish driver was killed at the Nürburgring in the 908/2 when it flipped over after losing one of the spoilers that helped keep down the nose. Elford and Ahrens won this event from Herrmann and Attwood in the Salzburg 908/3s.

The 917s were used for most of the remaining top races, but a Martini 908/2 driven by Rudi Lins and Marko took third place at Le Mans in 1970 behind two 917s. Tony Dean also drove a private 908/2 in Can-Am racing in America with some success.

Factory-prepared 914/6 GTs were entered for the Monte Carlo Rally in 1971, much against their drivers' wishes. They said the 911 was much faster with its better traction and ability to change direction more quickly because of its rear-hung engine. But the drivers were overruled by the works, desperate to boost sales. A disconsolate Waldegård could finish only third, when he had a hat-trick of wins in his sights.

PAGES 68/69 *Reinhold Jöst continued to campaign a team of 908/3s throughout the 1970s, fitting 2.1-litre turbocharged engines in 1975 from the 1974 Turbo RSRs. In this form, they became known as 908/4s. Herbert Müller is shown in third place at Spa before retiring with gearbox trouble.*

LEFT *Porsche Carrera RSR 3-litre prototypes took first and third places in the world's last great road race, the Targa Florio in 1973. The third-placed car, driven by Leo Kinnunen and Claude Haldi, is seen rounding one of the hundreds of corners on the tortuous Piccolo Madonie circuit.*

BELOW *Porsche 934s were produced in 1976 in Group 4 trim for GT racing to back up the more extensively modified 935s. This example, used by Mark Niblett/Charles Ivey Racing, features many 935 modifications.*

Martini took over sponsorship of the second-string works cars with 908/3s in 1971, although these models were only used in preference to 917s in the Targa Florio and the Nürburgring 1000 kilometres. Various troubles sidelined the 908/3s in the Targa, leaving Alfa Romeo to finish first and second; the 908/3s took the first three places at the Nürburgring, however, with Elford and Larrousse in the leading car. Most of the 908/3s were then sold to private customers, notably Reinhold Jöst, who campaigned his in various guises for years. He won the Kyalami Nine Hours in 1973 with Müller, putting Wyer's new Gulf into second place.

Porsche homologated the Carrera in 1973 to help Waldegård, who competed gallantly, but without success, in the East African Safari and the 1000 Lakes rallies. The Carrera paid off in circuit racing, however, when a prototype fitted with a 3-litre engine outlasted the Matras and Gulf-Mirages to win the Daytona 24-hour race for Peter Gregg and Hurley Haywood before they took it to Sebring and won again! This car, and another that had been raced by the Penske team, was then returned to Europe to be driven in Martini colours. One of these cars, fitted with 917 brakes and wheels, pulled off a shock victory for van Lennep and Müller in the Targa Florio as more powerful and lighter prototypes from Ferrari and Alfa Romeo crashed or retired. Van Lennep and Müller went on to take fourth place at Le Mans and give Porsche a totally unexpected third place in the world championship.

Porsche also made a habit of winning the GT category of the European Touring Car Championship at this time with 911s and Carreras entered by Kremer and Georg Loos. In 1973 the championship ended in a tie between Ballot-Lena and Clemens Schickentanz, with Britain's John Fitzpatrick winning in 1974.

The factory also prepared a special 911 RS 2.7-litre with raised suspension and special fittings for Waldegård to drive in the 1974 Safari. He thrilled everybody to lead for most of the rough, tough, event before suspension trouble put him back to second place near the finish. A new version of the Carrera RS was prepared for endurance racing using the

turbocharger system developed for the 917 in Can-Am racing. This was allowed to run in the 3-litre class because of its 2.1-litre capacity (a turbocharger being reckoned to be worth 1.4 times engine capacity). Several placings followed for its drivers, Müller and van Lennep, before they came within an ace of winning at Le Mans when all but a Matra broke down in front of them. This development car, run in Martini colours, took Porsche to another third place in the world championship.

Carreras continued on their winning ways with Hartwig Bertrams in the European Touring Car Championship GT class before Jöst 'borrowed' the turbocharged Carrera's engine for his 908/3 to carry on racing.

The 934, 935 and 936

During this year the works used the 908/3 and 917 as the basis for development of its new prototype racer, the 936. The Type 930 road-going Turbo was homologated as the 934 for Group 4 racing and extensively modified as the 935 for Group 5 events, which were to qualify for a revised World Championship of Makes. All these cars used turbocharged engines in 1976, and Jöst continued to race his 908/3 with Can-Am bodywork to win at the Nürburgring.

The Loos-entered 934, with a 480 bhp 3-litre engine classed as 4.2 litres, and with 917 brakes, won the European Touring Car Championship GT class for Toine Hezemans in 1976 as the works Type 935 disputed the World Championship of Makes. Its 590 bhp turbocharged engine was kept to a nominal 4 litres which worked out best in terms of minimum weight regulations. Despite fierce opposition from 700 bhp BMW 3.5 CSLs, the 935s took their world championship, winning every race except that captured by Jöst's 908/3.

The Type 936, which shared similar success in the World Sports Car Championship, had what amounted to a 908/3 frame with the 2.1-litre turbocharged engine and 917 brakes, gearbox and titanium drive shafts. Only one car was entered in each event, but, boosted by Jöst's 20 points for his victory in the 908/3, took the title as the more ambitious effort by Renault with the Alpine failed through unreliability or poor pitwork.

Ickx and van Lennep completed a virtual clean sweep for the year by winning at Le Mans in a 936 that led all the way except for the first few

RIGHT *Jacky Ickx and Gijs van Lennep led virtually all the way to win the 1976 Le Mans 24-hour race with their new Porsche 936. Rolf Stommelen and Manfred Schurti finished fourth in a 935.*

FAR RIGHT *The 936s that won at Le Mans in 1976 and 1977 ran again in 1979, leading until they were sidelined by electrical problems.*

BELOW *Jacky Ickx blew up his clutch on the line at Silverstone in 1976, lost 1¾ hours having it replaced, then broke the lap record chasing the field with his 935 for second to last place!*

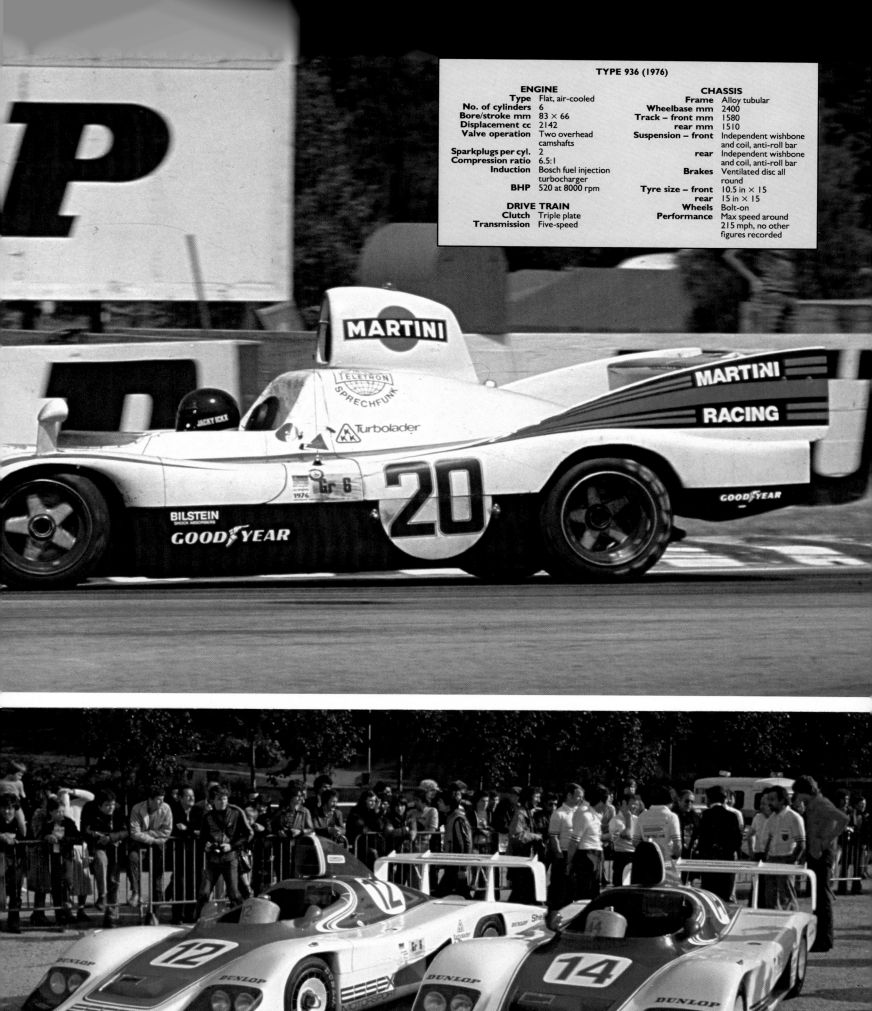

TYPE 936 (1976)

ENGINE		CHASSIS	
Type	Flat, air-cooled	Frame	Alloy tubular
No. of cylinders	6	Wheelbase mm	2400
Bore/stroke mm	83 × 66	Track – front mm	1580
Displacement cc	2142	rear mm	1510
Valve operation	Two overhead camshafts	Suspension – front	Independent wishbone and coil, anti-roll bar
Sparkplugs per cyl.	2	rear	Independent wishbone and coil, anti-roll bar
Compression ratio	6.5:1		
Induction	Bosch fuel injection turbocharger	Brakes	Ventilated disc all round
BHP	520 at 8000 rpm	Tyre size – front	10.5 in × 15
		rear	15 in × 15
DRIVE TRAIN		Wheels	Bolt-on
Clutch	Triple plate	Performance	Max speed around 215 mph, no other figures recorded
Transmission	Five-speed		

laps. Stommelen and Manfred Schurti finished fourth in a 935.

Porsche's chief rival in 1977, the French Renault team, concentrated on Le Mans, leaving the World Championship of Makes to the Germans. BMW put in only a token effort, however, and the Porsche people were among the first to admit that their clean sweep in the championship brought them little satisfaction. The Porsche works team, backed by Martini, ran 2.8-litre 935-77 cars with 630 bhp gained from twin turbochargers, which also almost eliminated the throttle lag problem.

Porsche derived a good deal more satisfaction from winning at Le Mans, which was not included in the championship. Renault desperately wanted to win here, having devoted an entire year's effort to the national race. And the French company looked as though it would win until all four works cars suffered from engine trouble, leaving the works 2.1-litre turbocharged 936 of Jürgen Barth and Hurley Haywood well in the lead. They were assisted by Jacky Ickx after his Porsche retired.

The Group 6 World Championship was an Alfa Romeo walk-over with no Porsche participation other than a token appearance by Jöst in his incredible 908/3.

The Porsche works team contested only two rounds in the 1978 World Championship of Makes, but it was still a walk-over. With only BMW for opposition, Porsche had the advantage of a full litre or more of engine capacity. The three-car Loos team won four times and the Kremer Brothers' solo entry three times with 3-litre 935-77As. The only race Porsche did not capture was at Silverstone, which was used as a shakedown for the works 3.2-litre 750 bhp 935-78. It took this event easily and went on to do battle with the Renault-Alpine team at Le Mans, in company with three Martini 936s.

Renault was bent on revenge, and got it with a new A443 prototype. This was the fastest car down the Mulsanne Straight—at 367 km/h (228 mph)—since the 917s had touched 386 (240). In 1978, the Porsche team was never able to contest the lead with the Renault-Alpines, and had to be content with second and third places for Bob Wollek, Barth and Ickx in a 936-78 and Haywood, Gregg and José Dolhem in a 936-77, behind the Alpine of Didier Pironi and Jean-Pierre Jaussaud.

In 1979, Le Mans was very much a case of Porsche against the rest; no fewer than 19 of the 55 starters were Porsches, with no Renaults. The two front runners were the Essex Petroleum-sponsored 936s for Ickx and Redman, Wollek and Haywood, with tremendous publicity for a private 935 driven by its owner, Dick Barbour, Stommelen and film star Paul Newman. The most interesting Porsche, however, was a very special 935 built by the Kremers, with bodywork modified to give a 'ground effect' like Formula 1 cars. This was called the 935K3 and was driven by Klaus Ludwig and the American brothers Don and Bill Whittington. The prototypes succumbed to tyre or mechanical troubles, leaving the 935K3 in the lead, which it held to the end, despite losing 14 laps with a broken fuel injection pump belt.

Porsche left a host of 935 customers to continue its cause in the World Championship of Makes in 1980 and 1981. As a result, Lancia won the title both years, with its 1.4-litre turbocharged Monte Carlos picking up maximum points in the smaller classes. Porsche 935K3s won numerous races, however, and Jöst rebuilt his 908 again with 936 bodywork as a 908/80 and nearly won Le Mans in 1980! Fuel pump and gearbox trouble delayed the car, driven by Jöst, Ickx and Michel Leclere, and they were narrowly beaten into second place by a French Rondeau. The Porsche

ABOVE *Fifty-four-year-old film star Paul Newman attracted the most publicity before Le Mans 1979 with his place alongside Dick Barbour and Rolf Stommelen in a 935. He drove consistently well to help move the car up to second place at the finish as faster machines broke down.*

LEFT *The 935K3 driven by Ludwig and the Whittington brothers stormed through torrential rain to win Le Mans in 1979. Their car had been modified by Erwin Kremer to improve aerodynamics and torque. It won despite losing 14 laps with mechanical problems.*

factory was more interested in promoting the 924 at the time, with a turbocharged version finishing a very creditable sixth.

When it was realized that Porsche could still win at Le Mans, the factory fitted the 2.65-litre turbocharged engine from the abortive Indianapolis project to a 936/81 with a 917 Can-Am gearbox for Ickx to try for his fifth victory, in 1981. This he duly recorded, beating the Rondeau, in partnership with Derek Bell. It was an especially happy day for them as they had won in 1975 with the Gulf prototype. Long-distance racing regulations were changed at the end of 1981 to a new Group C with an emphasis on fuel consumption, so that Porsche's interest was re-aroused. The 2.65-litre turbo engine was retained for a new monocoque car, the 956, for its shake-down before Le Mans in the Silverstone Six-Hour in 1982 in which it finished second with Ickx and Bell driving. At the same time, Porsche was developing a new 1.5-litre turbo V6 grand prix engine for McLaren with a Formula 1 debut scheduled in 1983.

RIGHT *Porsche planned an assault on the 1980 United States Auto Club's championship in conjunction with Ted Field's Interscope Team, whose driver, Danny Ongais, won at Daytona with a 935 in 1979. Porsche provided the power units for the car—2.65-litre developments of the 930's turbocharged flat-six, boosted to 630 bhp with methanol fuel for better cooling. The engine is pictured going on test with Ongais in a 1979 Parnelli chassis before installation in a new Interscope Porsche for the first race in Texas in April. The highlight of the USAC season is the Indianapolis 500-mile race. However, in late April the programme was cancelled by Porsche, as a result of a rule change which rendered the engine uncompetitive.*

The magnificent Porsche 917s

There is no doubt that the 917 was the greatest racing Porsche ever, and one of the most spectacular cars the world has seen. From the moment that Ferry Porsche gave the 12-cylinder project the go-ahead in 1968, world dominance of sports-car racing, with lap times faster than Formula 1 cars, was feasible. In essence, the 917 started as a 908/3 with half as much power again from the 4.5-litre engine and continued in its ultimate turbocharged form virtually to double that output at more than 1000 bhp. After problems in actually keeping the projectile on the ground in its first year of racing in 1969, it powered Porsche to a hat-trick of World Sports Car Championships under the inspired guidance of the Wyer team, and went on to achieve total dominance in the lucrative Can-Am racing in the United States and Canada in 1972 and 1973 in turbocharged form. Porsche was also lucky in having three of the greatest sports-car drivers of this era when unrestricted giants were let loose on a track: Josef 'Seppi' Siffert, Pedro Rodriguez and Mark Donohue.

The 917 was born of a decision by the Commission Sportive Internationale to outlaw the massive 7-litre Fords and Chaparrals from the World Sports Car Championship in 1968: in future the series would be contested only by 3-litre cars with a minimum weight of 650 kg (1433 lb) or homologated 5-litre cars with a minimum weight of 800 kg (1764 lb) of which at least 25 had been built. By framing the regulations in this way, the CSI was sure that the pure racing cars, with GP-style 3-litre engines, would have an advantage over the 'monsters' with stock-block engines. Surely nobody, not even Ferrari, Ford, Chevrolet (via Chaparral) or Porsche, had the resources to build more than 25 identical outright racing cars, such was the cost of construction and development? It was a challenge that Ferry Porsche accepted so that he could steal a march on his rivals, and

PAGES 76/77 *The 917 owned by Mark Finburgh, on show at Britain's Midland Motor Museum, is the short-tailed model formerly run by JW Automotive that Pedro Rodriguez drove to numerous victories in 1971.*

ABOVE *Gerhard Mitter gives the 917 its debut at Spa in 1969. He blew the engine while struggling to change into top gear.*

RIGHT *Stommelen storms into the lead at Le Mans with his long-tailed 917 in 1969. Team mate Elford took over the lead for the next 21 hours before both cars were eliminated with mechanical trouble.*

one that was to cost Porsche millions of marks, although much of this expenditure was recouped from selling the cars to customers and from an untold amount of invaluable development experience and publicity gained from such an exercise.

The alloy frame of the new 917 was almost exactly the same as that of the 908/3, except that the driver sat further forward to balance the extra weight of the 12-cylinder engine, which used the same bore and stroke as the 3-litre flat-eight in the 908/3. The chief difference, except for its size, was that the flat-12 took its power from the centre of the crankshaft to avoid whipping.

Suspension and brakes bore a strong resemblance to those of the 908/3, and there were similar long and short, coupé and spyder bodies, switched around to suit the circuit and races in which these cars were entered. This 'production' racing car created a sensation when it was unveiled in March 1969, and in the end only Ferrari could rise to the challenge and produce a direct competitor in the 5-litre 512 series.

The main problem with the 917 in 1969 was with aerodynamics: despite suspension-operated flaps like those used on the 908/3 and later banned, the 917 was notoriously unstable with its great power (around 560 bhp) and highly efficient streamlining. In the first year the road-hugging and highly manoeuvrable 908/3 was frequently more attractive to Porsche works drivers, although brave men such as Rolf Stommelen (with Kurt Ahrens) and Vic Elford (with Richard Attwood) fought for the lead at speeds approaching 370 km/h (230 mph) at Le Mans in 1969 after privateer John Woolf had been killed when he lost control of his new 917. Clutch trouble eliminated these duelling giants, leaving the field clear for the memorable battle between Ickx's Ford GT40 and the Herrmann/Larrousse 908.

The factory 917s were handed over to Porsche Salzburg and the clutches, oil cooling and braking improved, with Formula 1-style wide wheels fitted, in an attempt to improve the roadholding. The cars were still unstable, however, although Siffert and Ahrens coped with the 917 better than anybody to win at the Österreichring from Bonnier and Müller's Lola T70 with Redman and Attwood third in their 917.

Horsman's modifications to the 917

It was at this point that a brilliant English engineer, John Horsman, who ran the development and preparation side of Wyer's Gulf-sponsored team, got to work on the 917. He rejected the efforts of the Porsche technicians, led by Piech, who tended to concentrate on reducing drag, leaving the drivers to worry about keeping the car on the road. Horsman, who was quite capable of driving the cars himself, although he did not race personally, approached the problem with a fresh mind. He chopped off the 917's tail and built it up in shorter wedge-shaped form; this increased drag but saved weight and, more important, increased downthrust, which worked wonders for the car's stability. In one fell swoop, Siffert was far faster in the revised 917 despite its extra drag. The Porsche factory, which was providing technical support for the Wyer and Salzburg teams, promptly followed this line of thought with great success.

It was just as well because frantic efforts at Modena had resulted in a formidable big Ferrari lining up with the Porsches for the 1970 season. Rodriguez and Kinnunen, in the first Gulf Porsche, won the Daytona 24 hours with team mates Siffert and Redman second just in front of the Mario Andretti/Arturo Merzario/Jacky Ickx Ferrari 512S. Then Ferrari won at Sebring from Peter Revson and film star Steve McQueen in a 908/2 when the Gulf and Salzburg Porsches were eliminated by hub trouble or accidents. After that, the Porsches really got into their stride, winning most World Sports Car Championship races in the 917. Pedro Rodriguez, younger brother of Ricardo who had started racing in an RS, began the Porsche domination with one of his typically brilliant drives in soaking wet conditions at Brands Hatch. He simply drove away from the rest of the field, even though the Ferraris of Amon and Ickx and the

Salzburg 917 of Elford had been faster in practice.

The 917's engine was increased in capacity to 4.9 litres with 600 bhp for the next round of the championship at Monza, but Rodriguez still won in a 4.5-litre after problems with the new engine, and accidents. The 908/3 won the Targa, but it was back to the big Porsches for the very fast Spa circuit, where Rodriguez lapped at more than 258 km/h (160 mph), before retiring with a broken gearbox. Siffert was only fractionally slower and won with Redman, who had shared the winning Porsche in 1969.

The next event for the 917s, after the 908/3s had been used again at the Nürburgring, was Le Mans, with no fewer than eight Porsches disputing the overall lead with 11 Ferraris. In a race of attrition, Herrmann and Attwood lasted longest to win in a Salzburg short-tail 4.5-litre 917; and Herrmann promptly retired from racing after 20 years at the top. Siffert and Rodriguez left everybody else standing at Watkins Glen in the next round, duelling in the Gulf 917s, and Rodriguez won after Siffert's car had a puncture.

The 917 in Can-Am

The day after the Watkins Glen race the Swiss driver was back in action in a 917 to finish second behind Denny Hulme's 8.1-litre McLaren-Chevrolet in a round of the Can-Am championship. Attwood and Elford were third and fourth in the Salzburg 917s. McLarens had dominated this very lucrative form of racing, restricted by few regulations other than the necessity to have two seats, almost since its inception in 1966, but for the 1970 season Porsche had made a determined onslaught. Siffert did most of the driving in these races with a short-tail spyder designated the 917PA (for Porsche-Audi, sponsoring his efforts in Can-Am). Siffert's 4.5-litre 917 PA, backed by Tony Dean's 908/2, lacked horsepower compared with the 700 bhp McLarens, but took several placings; Dean actually won at Road Atlanta when everybody else broke down. It was also the first time Team McLaren had been beaten in 19 races.

Ferraris also gave some strong opposition in Can-Am racing, and Alfa Romeo nearly won the last round of the world championship at the Österreichring in their 3-litre prototype when Siffert had to nurse home his 917 after breaking a camshaft near the end.

So Porsche had won the world championship again and Le Mans at last. Such was the dominance of the 917 that the CSI decided to reframe its regulations from the end of 1971 in favour of the 3-litre cars. Although there was only one season to go, Porsche continued to develop the 917 for Wyer's Gulf-sponsored team, and Martini took over the Salzburg back-up squad. The company also kept a close eye on Can-Am, seeing it as a possible avenue of development and publicity, particularly as Porsche's fastest normal production car, the 911S, was severely handicapped in America by emission regulations.

The 917's engines were increased to a full 5 litres in experimental form; Ferrari gave up trying to compete in this sphere and concentrated on a new flat-12 3-litre prototype for 1972.

Wyer's Gulf team started well, winning the first round of the 1971 championship at Buenos Aires with Siffert and Derek Bell leading in Rodriguez and Oliver, from two Alfa Romeos. The team was lucky to win again at Daytona, however, as Rodriguez and Oliver's car survived a 90-

OPPOSITE *The Gulf 917 driven by Jo Siffert and Brian Redman won the Spa 1000 kilometres in 1970 with a new record average of 241 km/h (150 mph). Their car is seen here leading that of team mates Rodriguez and Leo Kinnunen who retired with mechanical problems—but not until Rodriguez had set a new lap record.*

LEFT *For Le Mans in 1970, Porsche revised the bodywork to make the long-tailed 917 more stable without sacrificing too much speed. This car, driven by Gérard Larrousse and Willi Kauhsen, also featured a controversial 'hippy'- style colour scheme devised for Martini. It was runner up to the 917 of Herrmann and Attwood.*

In 1970 Rodriguez had a great season in the 917—chassis number 013—now owned by Mark Finburgh, He won at Daytona, Monza, and Spa with Jackie Oliver, and the Österreichring with Attwood. The same car also won at Montlhéry with Derek Bell and Gijs van Lennep at the wheel. This car was subsequently used as the basis of a replica built by the German Kremer team, which proved quite competitive at Le Mans and in the World Championship of Makes in 1981!

minute stop in the pits for a gearbox rebuild. They went on to win after a brilliant drive in damp conditions by Rodriguez, who caught and passed the private Penske Ferrari 512M (a lightweight version of the 512S), which had spent 70 minutes having its suspension repaired. A Martini 917 driven by Elford and Larrousse won at Sebring after collisions delayed most of the opposition. By the fourth race of the championship at Brands Hatch, Ickx had put the new 3-litre 312P Ferrari on pole position, followed by Stommelen's Alfa Romeo. Fuel and hub problems delayed the 917s in the race and collision set back Ickx's Ferrari, with the result that Alfa Romeo won a world championship race for the first time in 20 years.

The Gulf and Martini 917s were back with a vengeance at Monza, as the 3-litre prototypes simply could not keep up on this very fast course. Rodriguez and Oliver won easily from Siffert and Bell. Wyer's men won again at Spa, with Siffert setting the fastest lap at 260.71 km/h (162 mph) and Rodriguez and Bell winning.

The 908/3s contested the next two rounds in the Targa Florio and Nürburgring events, and Le Mans presented quite a spectacle as 917s turned up in all manner of shapes. Many showed signs of Porsche experimentation with aerodynamics over the winter, and none more so than one to be driven by Willi Kauhsen and Jöst. It was painted pink with lines dividing it up like a diagram of pork cuts. This scheme derived from its factory nickname, the Schwein, gained from its short, stubby, nose. This form of snout was necessary to provide greater downthrust at the front to counterbalance the longer tail, which reduced overall drag. All manner of troubles beset the front runners, with the result that the 'factory reserve' 917 of Marko and van Lennep powered through to win.

Pedro Rodriguez drove the last great race of his life at the Österreichring when his Gulf 917 lost three laps with electrical trouble and he made a fantastic come-back on a damp and slippery track to win from the Alfas. Two weeks later he was killed in a crash when driving Müller's private Ferrari 512 in a non-championship event, and three months later Siffert died, too, when his Formula 1 BRM crashed in flames at Brands Hatch, after he had won the 917's last world championship race at Watkins Glen.

Porsche's greatest drivers had been lost, but the world championship had come to Zuffenhausen for the third time running. It was the end of an

ABOVE *Mark Donohue dominated Can-Am racing in 1973 with the fastest Porsche ever built, the long-wheelbase 917-30, seen here in company with the 911 Carrera RSR with which Peter Gregg won at Daytona that year.*

LEFT *Porsche built special spyder bodies for the relatively short-distance Interserie championship in 1971. This series appealed to customers whose 917s were uncompetitive in longer events. Kinnunen, seen here finishing third at Imola won the championship.*

era in which the very powerful sports cars competed in all manner of events. The 917 carried on, however, to achieve new heights of fame and glory in the shorter-distance Can-Am racing.

Siffert had driven a new form of 917 in Can-Am from the fourth round at Watkins Glen in 1971. This was the 917-10 with a snub nose developed from the Le Mans cars and many ultra-lightweight parts to keep its weight down to 740 kg (1631 lb). It was a good deal faster than the 917PA (still being campaigned by Milt Minter), and took Siffert to fifth place in the overall standings. It was obvious, however, that the 917 needed more power if it was to beat the giant-engined McLarens in 1972.

Penske forsook his Ferraris to run the works-assisted Porsche team with his brilliant driver-development engineer, Mark Donohue, in 1972. The extra power was supplied by turbocharging, at first to give 850 bhp in 4.5-litre form as the chassis needed development to take this much. Meanwhile customers' 917s had their engine capacities increased to 5.4 litres to give 660 bhp against the McLarens' 730 bhp.

The turbocharged 917-10 suffered a valve problem in its first race at Edmonton, then crashed at Road Atlanta, so George Follmer was called in to replace the injured Donohue. Follmer won three rounds for Porsche (with Donohue winning another when he recovered) to take the Can-Am

title in 1972. The previously all-conquering McLarens fought hard but just could not match the power and reliability of the 917-10.

Still more power was developed from the turbocharged Porsche in 1973 with a 5.4-litre capacity. Team McLaren tried to turbocharge a Chevrolet V8 but could not afford the development costs and withdrew from this form of racing; UOP-Shadow also tried a turbocharged Chevrolet with little success, so the 1973 season became a Porsche, Penske and Donohue benefit after minor problems in the first two races. Donohue's 917-30, with lengthened chassis and revised aerodynamics to cope with the extra power, won six races in a row, drawing ever further away from the rest of the field, which was made up mostly of turbocharged Porsches in any case. This led the SCCA to change the rules governing fuel consumption to outlaw turbocharged cars, a popular move in view of the energy crisis of 1973–4. A similar situation existed in Europe where the Interserie series (with regulations like those governing Can-Am) fell to Leo Kinnunen's Porsche for three successive years.

Porsche then retired honourably, but racing never seemed the same with the departure of the monsters that could outrun a grand prix car with their two speeds of 370 km/h (230 mph) achieved in Can-Am and 386 km/h (240 mph) at Le Mans.

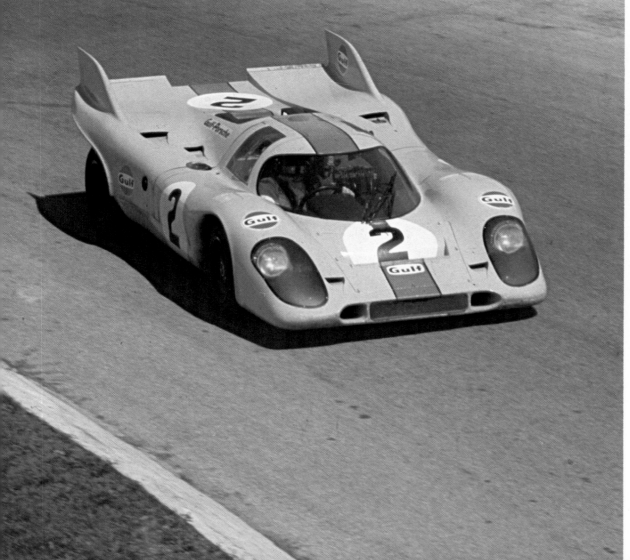

TYPE 917-30 (1973)	
ENGINE	
Type	Flat, air-cooled
No. of cylinders	12
Bore/stroke mm	90 × 70.4
Displacement cc	5374
Valve operation	Four overhead camshafts
Sparkplugs per cyl.	2
Compression ratio	6.5:1
Induction	Bosch fuel injection, twin turbochargers
BHP	1100 at 7800 rpm •
DRIVE TRAIN	
Clutch	Triple plate
Transmission	Four-speed
CHASSIS	
Frame	Alloy tubular
Wheelbase mm	2500
Track – front mm	1670
rear mm	1564
Suspension – front	Independent, wishbone and coil, anti-roll bar
rear	Independent, wishbone and coil, longitudinal links, anti-roll bar
Brakes	Ventilated disc all round
Tyre size – front	12 in × 15
rear	17 in × 15
Wheels	Bolt-on
Performance	Max speed around 230 mph, no other figures recorded

LEFT *Rodriguez and Oliver take the Midland Motor Museum 917 to victory at Monza in 1971. They were ably backed by the other Gulf team car, driven by Siffert and Bell, in second place with their nearest competitor, an Alfa Romeo T33-3 driven by Andrea de Adamich and Henri Pescarolo, six laps down. It was the start of the glory years for the 917.*

The latest Porsches
The 924s, 944 and 928s

Superficially, the latest Porsches look alike: the 924 and the 928 are both wedge-shaped coupés of relatively conventional lay-out with a water-cooled engine at the front and rear-wheel drive. In reality, they are poles apart, with the cheaper 924 using as many proprietary Volkswagen parts as possible and the 928 being pure Porsche, owing little to anybody else. This is because they were conceived together in the early 1970s as two separate sports cars with the 924 intended as a Volkswagen and the 928 as a Porsche. As it worked out in the end, the 924 only became a Porsche by accident.

There was nothing accidental about their design being so radically different from all previous Porsches, however. The use of a frontal engine position and water cooling rather than a rear engine and air cooling were the results of intensive research. In 1971, when basic lay-outs of the 924 and 928 were being worked out, the future of high-revving air-cooled engines, such as those used in the 911, looked bleak. They made too much noise, especially in alloy form, and that noise was concentrated in one spot at the back of a Porsche. Thus, with more stringent noise restrictions being introduced, particularly in Germany, it seemed wise to look for a quieter form of power. Water jackets absorb quite a lot of engine noise, so this form of cooling became attractive. Slower-revving engines also tend to be quieter, so a power unit of larger displacement (so that power should not be reduced) also seemed to be a good idea.

It was decided that the engine should be mounted at the front of the car for a variety of reasons. One was that the mid-engined lay-out, as in the 914, was showing itself to be a handicap when it came to usable interior space. A second was that if Porsches were to have a larger engine, its weight would be likely to cause severe problems if it overhung the rear axle. A third was that front-engined cars with their longer exhaust systems did not have the mechanical noise concentrated in one area in the manner of a rear-engined car. The noise tended to be divided between the engine and the exhaust system throughout the length of the car, which meant that it would not strike a fixed-position microphone, such as the type used in noise tests, with the same severity. A fourth reason was that concentrating a large mass of metal in the front of the car should make it easier to meet increasingly severe forward-impact tests in the United States. The fifth reason was that a frontal engine position gave more room to fit the exhaust-emission regulating devices that were being demanded by the American government.

Front-wheel drive was rejected because of handling problems associated with conveying large amounts of power through the steering wheels. Therefore the new cars had to be rear-wheel drive. A transaxle lay-out was chosen because it enabled the heaviest components, the engine and the transmission, to be located at either end of the car. This made it possible to achieve a near-perfect balance of 50 per cent frontal weight, 50 per cent rear, which was inherently better for handling and much better for straight-line stability than the rear-engined configuration. It also liberated the maximum amount of room for the all-important driver and front-seat passenger in a sports car, because there would be no large transmission hump to intrude between them.

This lay-out was decided for the new Porsche 928, intended as a replacement for the 911 series, before work started in earnest on the 914. It was used also for the 924 following marketing reports from Volkswagen, who had ordered a cheap, new, sports car from Porsche to replace the 914 and said that the new car should bear some family resemblance to the projected Porsche. Other requirements for the new Volkswagen sports car were that it should use an absolute maximum number of parts from the Wolfsburg range, not just some as in the case of the 914. This would keep down the cost. Price was all-important with the 924 as it was becoming apparent, from queues of up to a dozen customers for every used 911, that there was a big market for a cheaper German sports car. Porsche was happy at the thought of one of Zuffenhausen's designs meeting this need, rather than somebody else's. It had also been decided that the 924 should have more room inside and be more comfortable than the 914 to make it more popular for potential customers. All these factors influenced the Porsche designers as they worked on the 924 and 928 projects.

Although work had started first on the 928, the need for a new cheap sports car was more pressing, particularly as the 911 series had shown itself to be capable of being updated satisfactorily. The 2.7 Carrera and Turbo projects were ample evidence of this. Therefore, with 914 sales never really reaching target, the 924 was introduced first.

The 924

Volkswagen originally commissioned its design, but dropped the idea during a political upheaval and Porsche took over responsibility for production at the old NSU plant near Stuttgart. The 924 still showed considerable evidence of its links with Volkswagen, however, because that was the way it had been designed.

The 1993 cc engine was essentially the unit Volkswagen developed from the Audi 100 powerplant for its range of LT commercial vehicles. The chief difference between the four-cylinder water-cooled Audi and Volkswagen units was in the single belt-driven overhead camshaft in place of the Audi's pushrod valve operation. Porsche improved the engine

PAGES 86/87 *The outstanding Porche 928S introduced for 1980.*

RIGHT *The 924 and the 928 (in the background of the main photograph) might look alike, but in reality they are completely different cars. The 924 is a sports car built to a low-cost budget whereas the 928, with a similar wedge shape and water-cooled front-mounted engine, is a magnificent machine made with little more than perfection in mind, no matter what the cost. Nevertheless, the 924 is far from austere, as can be seen from its pop-up headlights that retract to present as little wind resistance as possible, and the mechanical efficiency of its engine which is also shown.*

further by raising the compression ratio to 9.3:1 and by fitting Bosch K-Jetronic fuel injection. The result gave 125 bhp, which, although not startling, was good enough for a small car with low drag and especially miserly fuel consumption. This unit was mounted well back in the engine bay, and canted over to the right to allow for a low bonnet line.

The transaxle, which used an Audi four-speed cluster, was connected to the power unit by a long torque tube, which also provided mountings for the gear linkage and exhaust system. The clutch was mounted at the engine end of the transmission to avoid the necessity of having two flywheels, one at each end of the propeller shaft. Lancia and Alfa Romeo had fitted clutches at the other end when using similar transaxles to make life easier for their synchromesh. These systems had the disadvantage of needing a more complex clutch linkage, however, so Porsche decided to avoid this problem and rely on the synchromesh. It was ironic that it was of the Volkswagen cone-type, not Porsche's own!

The transaxle lay-out had the additional advantages of spreading the load in the event of an accident severely affecting either end of the car, and allowing itself to be mounted relatively softly because of the distance between front and rear mountings. The main disadvantage was that it infringed on luggage space, but this had to be accepted.

The torsion-bar and trailing-link rear suspension was ingenious in its use of existing components from the Volkswagen range. It was basically the same as the 911's, except that it used parts from the Volkswagen Super Beetle! The drive-shaft joints came from the Volkswagen utility vehicle. The Beetle's coil-spring struts were used at the front, and were linked to wishbone arms from the Volkswagen Scirocco, or Rabbit as it is called in the United States. The steering was also Scirocco-based, and the brakes, disc front and drum rear, came from the Volkswagen K70 saloon. The use of drums at the back ensured that the 924 had a good handbrake at reasonable cost. To complete the puzzle, many of the smaller parts and interior fittings came from Volkswagen or Audi cars.

Although basically wedge-shaped, the 924 was made far more attractive by a careful rounding of the body lines and neatly faired-in bumpers allied with attractive wheels. Visibility for the driver and passenger also received a lot of attention with the result that the 924 was fitted with a large, opening rear window. Besides giving panoramic vision, it made luggage loading easier. Rear seats were fitted, but they were of enforced minimal dimensions because of the necessity of fitting a transaxle. Children up to the early teens could manage to squeeze into them, however.

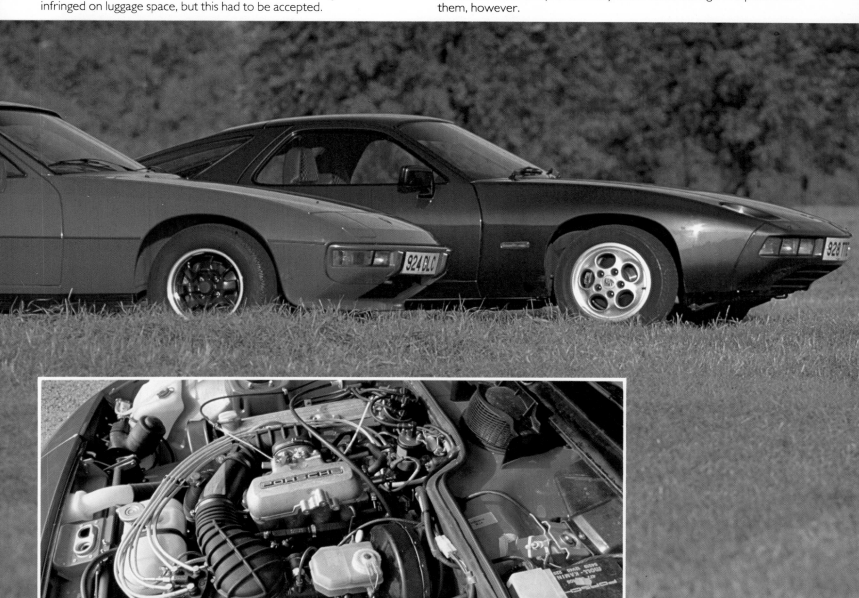

The introduction of the 928

The Porsche 928 introduced just over a year after the 924 was a different car altogether. It readily adopted the intended supercar image despite being more of a touring machine than an outright sports car. As such it complemented the 911 range rather than competed with it. Porsche chose a V8 engine because of the need to have a large power unit mounted in the front of the car. A low bonnet line was also necessary, but a flat-eight would have been too wide to give room for the front wheels to be swung round satisfactorily. The ideal compromise for a compact engine in terms of length, width and height was a 90-degree V8, so that is what Porsche designed. It was a brand-new all-alloy unit with considerably oversquare dimensions. A 95 mm bore and 78.9 mm stroke gave a capacity of 4474 cc with the bore dictating the other measurements. It was fixed at 95 mm to enable development to proceed in common with the 3-litre flat-six engines, which shared the same bore. Like the rest of Porsche designs for the 1970s and 1980s, it was intended to cope with any conceivable legislation so it had a relatively low compression ratio of 8.5:1 to allow it to be run on lead-free petrol. Ironically the cheaper 924 demanded higher-grade fuel because of its Audi ancestry! The new unit had a single overhead camshaft for each bank of cylinders in the interests of efficiency and to keep down the overall width and production costs. Twin overhead camshafts on each bank of a 90-degree V8 would have been impossibly wide, or the engine would have been too tall had the angle been narrowed. Hydraulic tappet adjusters were fitted to ease maintenance and promote quieter running and the camshafts were driven, in company with the water pump, by a cogged belt now that this form of propulsion had been proved reliable. The well-tried Bosch K-Jetronic fuel injection was used.

The clutch was fitted at the engine end of the torque tube in the same manner as on the 924, except that it was a twin-plate affair—which was very unusual at the time. This meant that the clutch was well able to absorb a lot of torque, but at the same time, by careful attention to its controls, was light in operation.

Although the 928 was fitted with a transaxle like that of the 924, it was fundamentally different in that the gearbox was ahead of the rear axle instead of behind it. The 924 had to compromise with its gearbox position because of availability of components, but no such compromise was necessary for the 928, so it had the gear clusters within the wheelbase for the best weight distribution. This also saved weight in that the propeller shaft and torque tube were shorter. In this way it was more like the established transaxles used by Ferrari than those of Alfa Romeo or Lancia. Direct drive was chosen for top gear, with Porsche synchromesh of course, rather than indirect as before, to keep down noise. The gear change reverted to the old Zuffenhausen lay-out with first away to the left and back with fourth and fifth gears in a direct plane. The reasoning behind this was that the V8 engine had so much torque that first gear would only rarely be needed, whereas it had to be used more often with the flat-six engine, hence its change on the 911 to a plane with second gear.

Daimler-Benz three-speed automatic transmission was offered as an option from the start in view of the car's touring appeal. Apart from being of German origin, the Daimler-Benz transmission was attractive to Porsche because it was of great mechanical efficiency, even if it was not quite as smooth as some American automatic gearboxes. This meant that the 928 automatic lost very little in performance compared to the manual edition. There was no question of the company building its own automatic gearbox: it was not big enough for that yet.

The 928 fitted with automatic transmission had the torque converter mounted at the gearbox end of the power train in the interests of efficiency, so a different body section was needed. The engine retained the same bell housing as on the manual version, but with only a ring gear for the starter to occupy it.

The 1979 928 shown in all its glory, V8 engine, alloy wheels and unique rear light clusters included: a car fit to stand alongside Porsche's 930 Turbo as one of the best vehicles in the world.

A great deal of research went into wheel control on the 928. Strut-type suspension systems or swing axles were rejected because of their imperfections in this sphere, so wishbones were used front and rear. In any case, their lay-out had been perfected on racing Porsches such as those described in the chapter on the 904s to the 936s. Aluminium was used wherever possible to reduce the unsprung weight, with coil springs because they were far less expensive than torsion bars and just as effective. Anti-dive geometry was built into the front suspension and an ingenious lay-out called the Weissach system (after Porsche's development ground largely set up for the 914 near Stuttgart) was fitted at the rear. This was an unconventional trailing-arm system that actually 'steered' to produce toe-in as the car slowed down. Normally trailing arm systems produce toe-out under such conditions, which leads to instability. And it was all done with rubber bushes!

Rubber, in the form of Pirelli P7 tyres, played a large part in the 928's development. These tyres really came into their own, with wonderful grip and handling, when the suspension's characteristics were developed around them. It was the painstaking sort of process at which Porsche engineers excelled. The steering received equally dedicated attention. A Porsche rack and pinion system was developed around a special ZF pump, with the result that its power assistance decreased with speed to produce the best of both worlds: plenty of power at low engine revolutions with plenty of feel as the power assistance decreased with the increase in the car's speed.

The 928's body was typically frugal in appearance, with no apparent bumpers. There are many people, the author among them, who appreciate this simplicity of line, but an equal number inquire, quite rightly, what would happen if something bumped into their precious Porsche? As ever, Porsche engineers had an answer: the 928's bumpers are hidden within the body and meet all stringent crash regulations. The actual body panels over them are one-piece plastic mouldings with 'elastic paint' that simply pop in and pop out with the bumpers!

The basic steel body shell (with aluminium bonnet, front wings and doors) was very strong with a built-in roll-over hoop, which also ensured sufficient rigidity to allow the fitting of an opening rear window.

The interior also belied the car's frugal appearance: the fittings were quite fantastic. The entire instrument panel moved up and down with the adjustable steering column and the pedals were adjustable too. A complete air-conditioning system was fitted that extended to the glove box should it be wished to pop a box of chocolates or some fruit in there! Tiny lights abounded everywhere: one was so angled as to illuminate the passenger's face without disturbing the driver should the vanity mirror be called into action at night; another was contained within the key ring to assist entry in the dark. A very comprehensive system of warning lights was fitted; there were some you could switch off for minor imperfections, and others that you could not switch off because they affected safety or legality. Two-stage windscreen-washing equipment was fitted to deal with any known kind of smear on the screen, and the rear window and exterior mirror were electrically heated in such a way that they could combat almost any combination of elements. Even the headlights had an interior hydraulic adjustment to counteract abnormal loading. The tiny rear seats folded down to give more luggage space and the magnificent front seats were the same as those on the 911 series.

It was the wheels that really set off the 928, though. They were beautifully sculptured from alloy to a futuristic pattern that complemented the simple lines of the body.

Automatic transmission became available for the 924 as an option nearly a year after its introduction, in October 1976. In addition, instrumentation was improved and rubbing strips added to the body sides, and soon after that, in January 1977, a special edition was produced. These cars had anti-roll bars front and rear, alloy wheels, and a leather-covered steering wheel, with Porsche-Martini factory racing colours of white, red and blue to commemorate the double world championship victories in 1976.

The most significant modifications made in 1978 were mounting the rear suspension on rubber to improve the ride and reduce the noise level, and offering a five-speed Porsche gearbox at extra cost (this the result of popular request).

For anyone who is money-conscious, the 1980 924 Turbo is an extremely attractive sports car, offering performance in the same league as most of the supercars, including the Porsche 928, at roughly two-thirds the price. Outwardly it is easily identified by its alloy wheels and rear spoiler lip. Inwardly the turbocharger is self-evident under the bonnet.

The 924 Turbo, 924 Carrera GT, 928S and 944

Far more dramatic changes were afoot for 1979. Porsche capitalized on experience with the 930 to turbocharge the 924 and give it 928-style performance at roughly two-thirds the price, or half the price of a 930. Cost consciousness aside, the 924 Turbo had more than a hotted-up engine: the running gear was changed in keeping with its power output, rising from 125 bhp to 170. A KKK turbocharger was tucked well down beside the engine, which had a special lower compression head and retained its Bosch K-Jetronic fuel injection. The bottom end of the engine was already strong enough to take the extra boost, but a new 911-style clutch had to be fitted with a stronger propeller shaft and torque tube and revised gearing. The 924 Turbo was also fitted with attractive new alloy wheels of 16 in diameter to take Pirelli's low-profile P7 tyres. An additional benefit that sprang from using these bigger wheels was that larger brakes could be fitted, with discs at the back to cope with the extra performance. Dampers were uprated, and steering ratio reduced.

Functional changes were made to the body with new grilles, four air inlets in the nose, and a NACA duct (named after the style of low-drag air intake used on American space probes) on the right-hand front wing. A spoiler was fitted at the back and altogether the 924 Turbo turned out to be a much more sophisticated car than the standard model.

Later in the year a Carrera GT version of the 924 was produced to test potential customers' reactions to proposed production in the 1980s. This was a development of the 924 Turbo with much weight saved by the removal of interior trim and the use of plastic and aluminium panels in place of steel in the bodywork. Power was increased to 210 bhp and the body shape modified to improve aerodynamics; alloy was used for the wider 15 in wheels, 178 mm (7 in) wide at the front and 203 mm (8 in) at the rear. Firmer suspension, a limited-slip differential and larger, ventilated, competition brakes were fitted to this sporting machine.

Meanwhile development continued on the 928 following its introduction early in 1977. The first major change was in the launching of the 928S model in 1979 to put this Porsche firmly in the world's supercar class with a performance almost as good as that of the 930. To achieve this, the 4.4-litre engine's liners were deleted to give 4664 cc from a 97 mm bore. As a result the power was increased from 240 to 300 bhp. Outwardly there was little to distinguish the two 928 Porsches other than the fitting of very restricted spoilers at the front and rear of the S type, and a new style of alloy wheel. The automatic gearbox was standard and the five-speed manual unit was optional as it was evident that the 928 was going to appeal mainly to the touring classes.

The culmination of all this development was revealed in the 944 introduced in September 1981. This was essentially a 924 Turbo with steel panels to give a lasting finish and a new 2.5-litre in-line four-cylinder engine based on one bank of the 928's. A prototype was impressive at Le Mans in 1981, finishing seventh. The 944 was expected to sell well in countries like the United States, where low-speed pulling power is more important than top speed, and the 924 Turbo in areas where taxation is severe on engines above 2 litres. The Carrera continued to be developed for competition as the 924GTR, with a 375 bhp turbo engine for circuit racing, and for rallying as the Carrera GTS with 280 bhp and revised suspension, with all-alloy bodywork. Further developments include anti-lock braking and a 924 turbo diesel engine for the ultimate economy and performance.

ABOVE LEFT *The latest in a long line of Porsches, the 944 has a power output of 163 bhp at 5800 rpm, which gives the car a top speed of 222 km/h (138 mph) with acceleration only slightly slower than the 924 Turbo.*

BELOW *The distinctive side view of Porsche's latest 928, the S model, which can be recognized by its new slotted alloy wheels and discreet spoiler around the rear window. Under the bonnet, however, is no less than 300 bhp against an original 240.*

Index

Acknowledgements

The publishers would like to thank the following individuals and organizations for their kind permission to reproduce the photographs in this book:

Geoffrey Goddard 56 above, 58–59, 62, 64–65, 78–79 above, 79 below, 80–81, 81 inset, 85 below; LAT 56 below, 57 inset below left, 59 right, 64 inset below, 66–67 below, 72–73 above, 74–75, 84 below, 84–85 below; Roger Manku 73 below, 75 above right; Porsche Cars (GB) Ltd 6 left inset, 10 inset, 75 below, 94 above; Snowdon and Associates 60–61, 66 above, 68–69, 70, 72 below.

All other photographs by Ian Dawson.

In addition, the publishers would like to thank Chris Branston and David Edelstein of the Porsche Club of Great Britain for all their help and assistance on this book. Thanks are also due to the owners who kindly allowed their cars to be photographed and to Mike Cotton of Porsche Cars (Great Britain) Ltd for providing road test cars.